Ferdinand Fellmann

Rethinking Georg Simmel's Social Philosophy

 Springer

Ferdinand Fellmann
(deceased)
Münster, Germany

ISSN 2212-6368   ISSN 2212-6376   (electronic)
SpringerBriefs in Sociology
ISBN 978-3-030-57350-8   ISBN 978-3-030-57351-5   (eBook)
https://doi.org/10.1007/978-3-030-57351-5

This Springer imprint is published by the registered company Springer Nature Switzerland AG.
The registered company address is: Gewerbestrasse 11, 6330 Cham, Switzerland

Introduction

Georg Simmel Up to Date

Georg Simmel (1858–1918) was one of the first German sociologists concerned with relationships—especially interaction—and was known as a methodological relationist. This approach is based on the idea that interaction exists in all facets of social life. Simmel was mostly interested in dualisms, conflicts, and contradictions in all domains of the social world. Strangely enough, Simmel, as the founder of relational sociology, is more present in American than in European sociology. Reservations on the part of his German colleagues are most likely due to the unprofessional aspects of Simmel's style of living and thinking. He lived in Berlin, in the cultural ferment of the period (from the turn of the century to World War I). His lectures at the University of Berlin were frequented by a broad public, mostly by intellectual women who were fascinated by the aura of Simmel's personality.

The German philosopher and journalist Theodor Lessing, put to death by the Nazis in 1933, criticized Simmel for producing a philosophy about everything, about the handle of a jug, about threshold, about flirtation, etc.: *Was nicht ist, wird ersimmelt*—"What does not exist is *Simmelized*." This witty modification of the Latin adage *quae non sunt simulo* sheds light on the varied topics Simmel happened to be working on. He did not have the sociologist's quantitative bent but looked at social facts intuitively from the subjective perspective of his ambivalent feeling of life.

In contrast to the research programs based on surveys and statistics, Simmel's method of selecting interesting phenomenon from the social world is nowadays more relevant than ever. The changing structure of the modern world is indeed an exciting time in sociological theory, which searches for new perspectives on individualization. Combining objectivity and subjectivity, Simmel pioneered the genetic method of research, which surpasses the positivistic collecting of data and paves the way for a new phenomenological and existential analysis of social life. I would like to refer to Simmel's method as "genetic sociology," in analogy to the genetic phenomenology of Edmund Husserl. "Genetic" is not to be understood in the biological sense as referring to genes but in the sense of becoming or of genesis [1].

Simmel's Philosophy of Life

Whereas American sociology is more interested in the formal aspects of social interaction, European philosophy of culture stresses the historical context and the personal frame of Simmel's social philosophy. His personality was dominated by erotic excitements draped by the veil of intellectualism. Simmel and his wife lived a bourgeois life; their home became a venue for cultivated gatherings in the tradition of the salon. The couple exemplified the intellectual marriage of the period, celebrating the freedom of independent partners, as Sartre and de Beauvoir did after World War II. This was a way to justify the newly gained sexual liberty. Simmel had a son with his wife and maintained a lifelong intimate relationship with the poetess Gertrud Kantorowicz. He had a daughter with Kantorowicz, but concealed her existence from his wife. Angela (1907–1944) was born in Bologna and was baptized Angi Bolzano. He did not want to meet his daughter, and the mother was not allowed to bring her daughter to their meetings. Simmel's attitude toward his daughter leaves open several interpretations. Margarete Susman, a good friend of Gertrud Kantorowicz, writes that Simmel felt guilty about not having a relationship with his daughter [2]. Although Simmel refrained from seeing his daughter, Susman claims, "this unspoken yet assumed secret, which Simmel kept out of love for his wife, slowly tarnished their beautiful marriage" [3]. A more psychological interpretation regarding the ambivalent nature of Simmel's personality could be that he was not ready to be confronted with his own unbound sexual drive.

Of course, I do not adhere to an outdated biographism. In light of this personal background, though, I hypothesize that sexuality, the most general and most private feature of personality, is at the root of all cultural forms for Simmel. His qualitative approach is centered on erotic love based on male–female polarity, which implies that man and woman are equal in right but different in character. In his late essay of 1918 entitled "The Conflict in Modern Culture" Simmel demonstrates how the sexual revolution enabled the cultural evolution to achieve a higher level in the relation between life and form: "Genuine erotic life in fact flows naturally in individual channels. Opposition is directed against forms because they force it into generalized schemata and thereby overpower its uniqueness" [4]. There is, however, one schema that unites the individual and the general side of life and that may therefore be called a transcendental schema: the schema of Eros.

In view of this erotic undercurrent, Simmel's image of humans is ambivalent. He always considers both sides of every human trait, which are related in dialectical reciprocity. His dialectical approach is multidirectional; it integrates facts and values and rejects the idea that there are hard, dividing lines between social phenomena and individual consciousness. Life is a continual flux, but this flux is often interrupted by unforeseen events and dramatic changes of mood. Simmel's late philosophy of life is therefore not as positive as that of the French philosopher Henri Bergson, whom he admired. Simmel considers not only the future of evolution but also the origins of culture. He is deeply concerned with both the conflicts and contradictions that make human existence difficult.

What This Book Is About

This book takes up the main topics of Simmel's thought as well as the different stages of its development. The topics are presented in their historical context, and their influence on other sociologists and philosophers, especially in Germany, is emphasized. Half a century ago, in his conclusion of the classical monograph *Georg Simmel* (1984, revised edition 2002), David Frisby traced possible lines of reassessment in the hope that this may take place in the near future. But Frisby's hope has not yet become a reality, despite the secondary literature published on Simmel in the last few years, e.g., Gregor Fitzi, Matthieu Amat, and David Ruggieri, among others [5]. The contributions highlight a certain aspect of Simmel's work, such as the cultural turn of modern social research or the defense of relationism against the reproach of relativism, but none are really groundbreaking because they refer to known topics that have been dealt with for some time now. This book is an attempt to show that a new look at Simmel is realizable in a field that lies outside the known topics of Simmel's sociology: Erotic life.

In the following chapters, Simmel's "view of life" (*Lebensanschauung*) is explicated using genetic-phenomenological descriptions. Sociologists bound to so-called social facts are unable to grasp the many different levels of social interaction that are working independently yet interlinked. Lower levels of existence do not lose their importance but continue to function as essential components in the higher levels. This bottom-up process is the "red line" of our investigation, which, in analogy to Simmel's empirical reasoning, tends to surpass itself. This study also includes an evaluation of his ideas from the point of view of modern cultural philosophy and philosophical anthropology.

The book starts with the cultural turn that made Simmel the founder of relational sociology. Instead of beginning with the isolated individual, Simmel emphasizes intimate relations as the fundamental stratum of human culture (Chap. 1). Forms of sociability is the topic of Chap. 2. These forms represent a higher level with new laws of interaction, but they lead back to unconscious processes, and the phenomenon of seduction in its broadest sense is highlighted. The relation of seduction to the fall in Judeo-Christian tradition is particularly important for understanding Simmel as a Jewish thinker. European and American forms of culturalization are compared in Chap. 3. The new attitude of the USA toward Europe is discussed in terms of the current value discussion, which leads back to Simmel's concept of objective values. Chap. 4 presents Simmel's complete treatment of sex and intimacy in view of what he calls "real erotic life," which has a utopian tint. The development from sexuality to eroticism is considered the main presupposition of Simmel's view of modern culture. Eroticism plays a significant role in metropolitan life, according to Simmel, which has brought about great changes in the lifestyles of both men and women and has affected their self-validation. How identity and individuality interact is discussed in Chap. 5. Simmel's concept of personality leads to a higher level of human belief in light of the idea of the personality of God. The highest level of the process of individuation is ethics. From the genetic point of view, Simmel rejected the categorial imperative of Immanuel Kant's moral philosophy. The transformation of normative ethics into the law of the individual is the climax of Simmel's late philosophy of life (Chap. 6).

Simmel never presented his thoughts as a system; he communicated his ideas in stand-alone fragments. For example, his analysis of flirtation, which he views as the alternation between consent and refusal, seems to have no connection with his law of the individual. Upon closer inspection, though, it becomes clear that flirtation is not only evident in the coquette, but also in the attitude that corresponds to individual ethics. Seen as a whole, all these topics are finally brought together in Simmel's image of the human as a conflictual and ambiguous being in need of existential justification. Simmel's programmatic formula "from more life to more than life" refers to any form of human interaction beyond mere self-preservation. In modern society, erotic and aesthetic experiences combine, a mixture that becomes synonymous with the ultimate level of human culture. Finally, Chap. 7 is intended to be read as a summary of Simmel's cultural anthropology and philosophy of life, neither of which has lost relevance.

References

1. Daniel Sousa, "Phenomenological Psychology: Husserl's Static and Genetic Methods," *Journal Phenomenological Psychology,* 45, pp. 27–60 (2014).
2. Margarete Susman, "Erinnerungen an Georg Simmel," in Kurt Gassen, Buch des Dankes an Georg Simmel. Briefe, Erinnerungen, Bibliographie. Zu seinem 100. Geburtstag am 1. März 1958. (Berlin: Duncker & Humblot, 1993).
3. Ibid., 282.
4. Georg Simmel, "The Conflict in Modern Culture," in Donald N. Levine, *On Individuality and Social Forms* (Chicago: University of Chicago, 1971), 389.
5. See Gregor Fitzi, *The Challenge of Modernity. Simmel's Sociological Theory* (New York: Routledge, 2019); Mattieu Amat, *Le relationisme philosophique de Georg Simmel* (Paris: Honore Champion, 2018); Davide Ruggieri, *La sociologia relationale di Georg Simmel* (Mimesis, 2016).

Contents

Chapter 1
Sociology Reconsidered

1.1 Simmel's Formal Sociology

Simmel's theory of society is known as "Formal Sociology" (*Formale Soziologie*). Leopold von Wiese explains that "formal sociology" (the term was introduced later by his colleagues) results from Simmel's view of sociology as a theory of the forms of socialization. Simmel did not distinguish between formal and material sociology but emphasized the organizing aspect of social forms as the pivot of a new kind of sociology. The genetic method transcends mere descriptions of the intentional structures of interaction. It deals with subjects such as the phenomenological notion of the self; the creation of personal identity in an intersubjective space; and the analysis of passive geneses in the stream of consciousness. The genetic method enabled Simmel to plunge into layers of human existence that are pre-reflective, passive, and anonymous, though nonetheless active. His aim was to construct an all-encompassing social theory distinguished from the existing specialist sociologies.

In the early twentieth century, Simmel was assigned to a group of thinkers (next to Ferdinand Tönnies and Alexander Vierkandt) whose research was strongly influenced by psychology and philosophy [1]. Simmel was criticized in particular for not conceptualizing the normative aspect of social action. It is indeed undeniable that Simmel worked intuitively and took an aesthetic approach [2]. Von Wiese, who adopted Simmel's theory of the forms of socialization, regrettably states that Simmel lost sight of method in the last years of his life. But this does not mean his focus on the emergence of social forms has lost relevance. Even von Wiese acknowledges that evolutionary psychology could help us to understand the process of individuation [3]. What many interpreters perceive as aestheticism (i.e., an antagonist to realism) is actually a methodological turn away from sociological positivism, for instance, as developed by Emile Durkheim. Durkheim's endeavor to liberate sociology from psychological concepts was pioneering but could not account for community, which consists of cooperating individuals who feel good together. To cope with this phenomenon, Durkheim postulated a "collective consciousness" in which higher forces are at work over individuals [4, 5]. But this did not solve the problem of human connection; it merely pushed it into the metaphysical realm. Ethnologists like Ruth Benedict and Margaret Mead have therefore rejected the concept of collective consciousness, claiming that it is unusable for fieldworkers.

In opposition to Durkheim, Simmel's object of psychosocial analysis is the various forms of relations between humans of various group sizes. As Simmel wrote in "The Problem of Sociology" (1894) and presented in his lecture "Sociology of Social Life" (*Soziologie der Geselligkeit*) at the first Sociology Conference in 1910, under "formal" he understands the way in which interaction is experienced by those involved. Social forms function as the medium of communication, independent of the contents of communication. According to Simmel, form and function belong together, and the dynamic of social development should be emphasized. Underlying this dynamic is not the idea of progress, it is not teleologic in the sense of having a fixed outer purpose; rather, it results from interaction itself. Here, the principle of reciprocity becomes effective and includes concretely the exchange of goods as well as the reciprocal consent to exchange, which then acquires mental value or significance. Simmel thus incorporates a normative moment into the concept of society, one which Durkheim cannot grasp with his concept of collective consciousness. Simmel rejects the universalism of rationally grounded moral norms yet notes the ethical component of formalization. Motives and calls to action are the results of forms of behavior that are not rational but nonetheless effective.

Simmel uses the term *Wechselwirkung* (reciprocity) in two senses. The first points back to the conception of truth that Simmel developed in *The Philosophy of Money*. He uses the term *Wechselwirkung* in the sense of a mere logical relation of elements. Concerning social life, reciprocity means the concrete interaction of individuals. This double meaning has been derived from the early writings of the German logician Hermann Lotze (1817–1881), who was well known to Simmel. In 1886/1887 Simmel gave lectures on Lotze's practical philosophy. In the third book of his *Logik* (1874) Lotze states that every relation is based on the fact that different contents through internal reciprocities are registered in the mind [6]. This is the logical meaning of relation as a mental action. This formal relation is founded in a concrete relation, namely in the acting and suffering of individuals in interaction. This distinction has been adopted by Simmel in the step from the meaning of truth to the meaning of social reality as the ceaseless interaction of its members. Thus *Wechselwirkung* is to be translated in English as a logical relation or as interaction according to the context.

This double meaning of reciprocity was confirmed later by Arnold Gehlen, the most influential sociologist and anthropologist of the twentieth century in Germany. Gehlen defined culture as the totality of goods created by humans, both material goods and those of a mental nature. The most important form is the form of action that provides contents. These forms stabilize the subjective sensory overload, they generate imperatives. Gehlen expresses the normative function of form using the words, "Forms are the food of faith" [7]. Gehlen, who studied with Max Scheler, is therefore in agreement with Simmel, but his main focus on institutions is no longer acceptable for modern individualism. Predictable structures are obviously necessary for living in groups, but they must remain open to the spontaneity of informal groups if the institution is to avoid losing sight of social reality. Here, Simmel's attempt to maintain the creative potential of life in the forms of socialization was groundbreaking. His self-assessment was correct that his "Problem of Sociology" opened up a new field, namely "the theory of the forms of socialization as such, abstracted from their contents" [8].

Simmel developed his theory of the forms of socialization in view of Europeans and hardly took into consideration the research on simple societies by ethnologists. This restriction explains why Simmel's concept of society focuses on how humans who are highly developed live together economically and technologically. Simmel's *The Philosophy of Money* makes evident how the introduction of money gave modern society a dynamic that grants individuals a great deal of elbow room. In simple societies, according to Simmel, the role of the individual is subordinate to society, whereas in modern society a dialectical relation emerges between individuals and societies. Owing to the dialectic complexities of social life, sociology becomes more philosophic, if not speculative.

Simmel's idealistic concept of sociology was discussed by the German sociologist Siegfried Kracauer (he was later known for his work in film theory) in *Soziologie als Wissenschaft* (1922). In this early text, Kracauer seeks to establish sociology as a strict empirical science. The following passage is a central passage of his essay, which has not yet been translated into English:

> It is worth taking the time to consider the presuppositions of Georg Simmel's "sociology." This thinker, whose value for sociology is undeniable, distinguishes, for conceptual clarification, between the content and the form of social phenomena. He refers to forms as the accumulated generalizations of experienced reality in its separate moments, the selection of which is based on the central sociological idea. The expression "form" has an exact definition in the domains of social life (customs, ceremonies, internal regulations, social practices, etc.: all are social forms in a very concise sense), which is somewhat covered up by the way Simmel uses the term. More importantly, though, Simmel does not clarify how many of the forms he names interact, how they are layered, whether an objective look at their components on the sociological continuum is possible or not, etc. If one takes a closer look at the form-categories, which serve as the point of departure of sociological studies, then one recognizes that they, on the one hand, represent concrete beings of a mostly middle tier (e.g., "the poor," "the strangers") and on the other isolate abstract moments in which some sort of mode of existence of such beings become independent (e.g., the intersection of social circles). Simmel is not aware that many of his forms sink back into the contents of general forms (stated precisely: to specifications of higher generalizations), nor is he aware of the consequence of such an ordering of forms in the hierarchy of beings on the objectivity of related intuitions. Since he takes the middle layer as representative, staying close to their experience of reality and hardly ever ascending to the upper social categories, his studies are missing an axiomatic foundation; rather, they deal predominately with cognitions based on subjective descriptive psychology, which are often viewed as exceptional since they are obtained through the closest observation of their object. Such fruitful approaches to a new (material) epistemology are frequently found in Simmel (I am also counting his repeated mention of the problem of "distance"), he never actually saw the profound problematic in his sociological research [9].

In this passage, Kracauer distances himself from Simmel's plurality of forms, which are alienated from concrete phenomena. Subsequently, Kracauer stresses in the third part of his essay (entitled *"Problematik der Soziologie"*) that objects create concepts and not the other way around. Here, too, his opposition to Simmel's philosophical approach to sociology is evident. On the other hand, Kracauer's descriptions of certain social facts are not completely distant from Simmel's idealistic orientation. In the passage *"Hotelhalle"* of his philosophical treatise *The Detective Novel* (1922), Kracauer calls the hotel room a secularized church room, and finds that this interpretation is confirmed by Simmel's definition of society and his philosophy of life [10]. Despite his criticism of the idealistic approach, Kracauer positively mentions Simmel's cultural turn in sociology. And in the 1960s in his *Theory of Film,* Kracauer refers to Husserl's genetic phenomenology and spotlights futile subjects, which Simmel also practiced in his descriptions of the everyday phenomena of life.

1.2   The Cultural Turn in Sociology

Culture is a key concept for Simmel, and, as Margaret Susman writes, it even carried religious meaning for him [11]. But culture, for Simmel, was not like Hegel's "objective Spirit," which moved about in a higher realm, above social life. Culture is nothing outside of interaction, it is the form of living together represented by social relations. Simmel's concept of culture thus involves the logic of relations underlying human cohabitation. One could even speak of an "open culture" in analogy to Karl Popper's "open society."

As Simmel's thought develops in his later writings, he considers society nearer to culture in all its aspects. Although the analysis of social facts dominates his sociology, whereas cultural forms dominate his philosophical writings, a rigid separation is not to be found. Simmel does not consider society as an institutionalized structure but is concerned with the emergence of social forms resulting from interaction between individuals to satisfy emotional needs. A consideration of cultural forms draws our attention to the conditions necessary for interaction to develop among individuals. Interaction generates archetypical forms of all human sociality, called "patterns of culture" by Ruth Benedict. As Benedict put it, "Cultures from this point of view are individual psychology thrown large upon a screen" [12]. This applies to Simmel as well, whose emphasis on the role of culture in producing character and social rank gave hope to strangers and the socially underprivileged.

In his famous book on economic sociology, *The Philosophy of Money,* Simmel distinguishes between two forms of culture: subjective or personal culture and objective culture. Subjective culture as the domain of authentic individuality has priority. Despite the primacy of individuality, subjective culture is not self-contained. It can only develop with the help of objective factors, especially money. In the world of money, the individual is less bound to subjective moods which could prejudice his perception and evaluation of the given. Thus, objective culture may be defined as the road to common sense. Simmel appreciates the process of objectivation in the course of history but he was worried about the threat to individuality through the increase of objective social structures such as legal systems, technology, money, etc. In subjective experience, it is emotionality that provides the very basis for life to attain its self-transcending character beyond its institutional forms. "From more-life to more-than-life" is Simmel's well-known formula to describe this transition to a higher dimension of culture. The driving force of cultural evolution could well be called libidinous, in the specific sense of the energy in the will to live as well as in the broader sense of spiritual evolution. The growing process of the emergence of the individual from the group, which Simmel called "individuation," seems to have reached its peak in modern capitalism.

Doubtlessly, objectivity lacks empathy and makes personal communication difficult. Objective culture tends to be a runaway process leaving behind any subjective experience and empathy. Nevertheless, Simmel does not quite say that objective culture has an overall negative effect. On the one hand, to the extent that the circulation of money increases, the individual's emotional self-awareness decreases. Personal identity is fragmented and dissolved into a network of exchange governed by quantifiable monetary value. On the other hand, paradoxically, this results in greater potential freedom of choice for the individual, as money can be deployed toward any possible goal. Money's homogenizing nature encourages greater liberty and equality. The ambivalence of money and sex comes to light in prostitution, the structure of which is explained extensively in the chapter "The Monetary Equivalent of Personal Values" [13]. The analogy between money and sex is known, but the analogy between money and prostitution is surprising and typical of Simmel's view of life. Prostitution degrades the woman and reduces her intimacy to an impersonal exchange good yet protects privacy, thus making possible exceptional, incommensurable achievements in the art of love.

In the essay "The Concept and the Tragedy of Culture" (1911) Simmel argues that cultural forms emerge in social interactions and become fixed. As such they exist in perpetual tension with ongoing life processes, which tend to break off from old forms and create new ones. Thus, the concept of culture implies that the mind ("*Geist*") creates objective entities through which the development of the subject finds the way to self-consciousness and self-validation. This is the normal course of life. The continual creation of new forms is sometimes stopped by the rigidity of old forms. And this is the point where the cultural process becomes tragic. Romeo and Juliet as archetypical young lovers are the best example. The real tragedy of culture consists in exactly this: destructing forces directed against an entity arise from the deeper stratum of the entity itself. The structure with which human life has built up its own positivity becomes self-destructive negativity [14].

In a later essay, "The Conflict in Modern Culture" (1918), Simmel speaks about "conflict" instead of "tragedy." Although the schema of life-form dualism is maintained, the shift from tragedy to conflict shows modern culture more positively. The key concept in this essay is "life" in its cultural sense. Simmel was increasingly fascinated by the immediacy of experience, which he made relevant in contrast to sociological rationalism. This life-concept is not falsifiable, but "life" serves a heuristic function for models of social organization, which Simmel described systematically as the dialectic of life and form. "Culture" no longer stands for the superiority of mind over matter but for the endangering of humans through their own works. Simmel now joins the circle of European thinkers who perceived their own time as a crisis of culture and thus bade farewell to every form of cultural optimism (comparable to Sigmund Freud, who declared the discontent of culture).

For Simmel, human life is always connected to opposed qualities or tendencies stemming from an originally undifferentiated unity:

> Whenever life progresses beyond the animal level to that of the spirit, and the spirit progresses to the level of culture, an internal contradiction appears. The whole history of culture is the working out of this contradiction. We speak of culture wherever life produces certain forms in which it expresses and realizes itself . . . These forms are frameworks for the creative life which, however, soon transcends them [15].

Conflict is essential for change in spiritual life, that is, "struggle in the absolute sense of the term which encompasses the relative contrast between war and peace" [16]. Simmel considers conflict and reciprocity as two closely related forms of interaction. Continual morphogenesis is a leading idea in Simmel's later philosophy of culture.

Emphasizing the continual change of cultural forms, Simmel anticipated the "cultural turn" in philosophy, which is nowadays understood as the intellectual turn to the forms of life. The dissolution of cultural identities, their separation from closed societies, turns culture into a concept of reflection connecting empirical and transcendental moments. It is not only a matter of the cognitive aspects of social behavior but of what ethnologists have called the "feel of culture" (*Gefühlseindruck*). Even when Simmel distances himself from psychology, he still cannot neglect the role of emotional life in his depiction of interpersonal relations. Hence, he paved the way for the diffusion of culture into the life-feeling of individuals and communities.

Culture understood as the inclusive concept of all life values—which humans obtain through their mental work on what has been given in nature—is the outcome of cultivation. Underlying culture is a special form of interaction in which humans cultivate themselves in the same way that they cultivate things, i.e., they separate themselves from inborn behavior patterns and thus gain freedom. With the individualization of cultural forms, Simmel follows the definition of culture given by the founder of English social anthropology, Edmund Tylor, in 1871; culture is "that complex whole which includes knowledge, belief, art, morals, law, custom, and any other capabilities and habits acquired by man as a member of society" [17]. This holistic approach has been confined to introspection in Germany in any case. For Nietzsche, for instance, the social virtues like bravery, endurance, and obedience do not count as "true culture," which is primarily based on the mind and education and is manifested in the "unity of artistic style" [18]. Simmel is in a certain way also under the spell of this aesthetic concept of culture, but he frees himself from the "unity of artistic style" through the diversity of life forms and lifestyles that are to be found in modern societies and influence human mentality.

In light of the deconstruction of the traditional concept of culture the question of unity or diversity becomes acute, which is significant for the contemporary cultural transformation. In the meantime, a diversity of perspectives has taken hold. On all levels of social life there are polarities at work which determine the construction as well as the deconstruction of culture. Simmel's dialectical understanding of culture sheds light on how cultural identity is experienced *today*. Whereas traditional culture and social or state-order belonged together in the past, the external conditions of cultural unity are no longer applicable in the age of globalization. Comparable in linguistic and religious convictions, different cultures are divided in one and the same society. Multicultural societies emerge through mutual relations. This corresponds to the liberalism of pluralistic democracy, which speaks of cultural diversity without giving up the concept of society.

The more digitalization of the different social systems pushes us into *One World*, the clearer it becomes that "culture" exists only as symbolic form. This might sound like cultural pessimism, but there is also a positive perspective that Simmel emphasized in *The Philosophy of Money*. Economic exchange stands for basic human needs that want to be satisfied in all societies: it is the striving for sustenance, stable cities, and social security. Much points to how modern industrial societies fulfill the needs that were once the focus of traditional societies. As money and transactions increase, the individual is drawn into a network of exchange governed by quantifiable monetary value. This aspect becomes clear in Simmel's analysis of matrimonial ads, which he regards as one of the greatest representatives of modern culture. Matrimonial ads are a special case of the monetary expression of personal values because they shed light on the fact that intimate relationships are more and more sought via the internet.

The paradoxical interconnectedness of nearness and distance is prefigured in Simmel's depiction of modern society: a tissue or web of personal interactions. Especially the urban lifestyle that Simmel considered to be the motor of modern culture confirms the shift to the public exposure of privacy. To be sure, the origin and goal of the cultural process is unknown. Thus, one can conclude with Simmel that cultural sociology can only verify that the new world is made up of virtual realities whose members draw their values pragmatically from social networks.

1.3 Sociology of Religion

For a better understanding of Simmel's cultural turn in sociology, it is instructive to consider the function of religion in society. Religion in modern societies has its institutional place in the churches of different confessions. From the cultural point of view, however, religious belief is universal, and subjective religious emotions are closely connected to society as a whole. In Simmel's view life-feelings always have a religious underpinning. What is more, an erotic dimension underpins the religious sense. This is particularly true even in post-modern secularized societies. Therefore, Simmel's distinction between religion as part of objective culture and religiousness as an expression of subjective culture corresponds to his fundamental life-form dualism. In this sense religiousness is considered a priori to society, and the transcendental view makes Simmel a representative of the philosophy of religion in contrast to theology.

In America the view has been widely held that sociology is concerned with social institutions, which are defined as systems of common convictions and emotional attitudes and are mainly represented by churches. Against this background it is not surprising that Simmel's essay *A Contribution to the Sociology of Religion* was translated in English and published in 1905 in the *American Journal of Sociology.* This sheds light on the cultural orientation of the American intellectuals at the turn of the century. The founder of the journal, Albion W. Small, was very interested in the impact of religious sects on society. Simmel's effort to give sociology a firm methodological foundation and his role in general sociology were only recognized after the intervention of Robert Ezra Parc. Although the reception of Simmel's work in the second half of the twentieth century was subject to fluctuations, his methodology and categories of social interaction were generally adopted by culture-oriented sociology. This is the case with Erving Goffman. It was remarked 20 years ago that "Erving Goffman may become the unacknowledged reincarnation of Georg Simmel" [19]. This statement has proven to be true; Simmel is now explicitly acknowledged and his contribution to the justification of social research is recognized.

Simmel's essay "A Contribution to the Sociology of Religion" is a good starting point for understanding his transcendental philosophy of culture because it contains his view of socially regulated interpersonal relationships. Despite the all-pervasive rationalization of faith in modern society emphasized by Max Weber, Simmel stresses the permanence of religious feeling in culture. He writes:

> We can safely assume that many human relations harbor a religious element … All religion contains a peculiar admixture of unselfish surrender and fervent desire, of humility and exaltation, of sensual concreteness and spiritual abstraction, which occasion a certain degree of emotional tension, a specific ardor and certainty of the subjective conditions, an inclusion of the subject experiencing them in a higher order—an order which is at the same time felt to be something subjective and personal. This religious quality is contained, it seems to me, in many other relations, and gives them a note which distinguishes them from relations based upon pure egoism, or pure suggestion, or even purely moral forces [20].

In this passage the dialectical structure of religious feeling disclaims the mystical desire for a perfectly harmonious social world. The world-form of religiousness corresponds to the conflict between vital needs and moral ideals, a tension which nevertheless is the source of the development to a higher level of sentiments.

> Another side of the social life which develops into a corresponding one within the religious life is found in the concept of unity. That we do not simply accept the disconnected manifoldness of our impressions of things but look for the connections and relations which bind them into a unity; yes, that we everywhere presuppose the presence of higher unities and centers for the seemingly separate phenomena, in order that we may orient ourselves aright amid the confusion with which they come to us, is assuredly one of the important characteristics of social realities and necessities [21].

Religion is organized in churches or sects that are in apparent institutional contrast and competition. In contrast to this, Simmel observes that the subjective factor turns out to be the source of a non-competitive form of faith and a more encompassing unity of mental life. Simmel considers this unity not a substantial one but the result of social interaction. This means that religion is more than a mere feeling. Religion is rather the attempt to express human longing for the Absolute which is personified in God. Hence, the social relevance of religion is to sustain society. Religious belief is a way to connect the multiple aspects and purposes of human life that lack conceptual and logical coherence.

> The emotional value of religion—that is to say, the most subjective reflexive effect of the idea of God—is entirely independent of all assumption about the manner in which the idea originated ... We here touch upon the most serious misconception to which the attempt to trace ideal values historically and psychologically is exposed ... For, just as genuine and deepest love for a human being is not disturbed by subsequent evidence concerning its causes—yes, as its triumphant strength is revealed by its survival of the passing of those causes—so the strength of the subjective religious emotion is revealed only by the assurance which it has in itself, and with which it grounds its depth and intensity entirely beyond all the causes to which investigation may trace it [22].

Simmel's statement that religiousness is an end in itself holds true for erotic emotions as well. The close relation between religion and sexuality has been a common topic of social research in Germany, as can be seen in the classic book *Religion und Eros* (1941) by Walter Schubart. Simmel is convinced that the statement of empirical facts does not disturb the consideration of spiritual needs and that the sociology of religion and philosophy of religion are compatible. This compatibility is characteristic of Simmel's unity of method. Whether he is examining a social process, a type of emotion, or a historic individual, the logic of Simmel's procedure is always the same, namely, to show how the multiplicity of elements turns out to be coherent when the complex form of reciprocity is disclosed. Simmel makes an effort to balance the two sides of religious consciousness, subjective and objective, psychological and social, individual and collective.

An exposition and an analysis of Simmel's social philosophy of religion would require a longer essay. It may suffice to briefly mention the further development of the pluralistic view on religion in Germany, where there was a revival of Simmel in the last decades of the twentieth century. Similar to Odo Marquard, who pleads for a modern polytheism that would overcome monotheism, Simmel pleads for different religious attitudes among believers and nonbelievers alike. This tolerance is not a sign of indifference but the result of the universality of Christianity. Simmel writes, "It is only the Christian God who encompasses both believers and nonbelievers. Of all the powers within life, he is the first to break out of the exclusivity of the social group" [23]. This argument is characteristic of Simmel's dialectic view of human life. Different qualities or tendencies stem from an originally undifferentiated source, in the case of religion from the universal religiousness of human sociality. To put this process in a succinct formula: Religious plurality through individuation. Looking back, it is evident that Simmel's individual pluralism was developed by post-modern thinkers who adopted genetic phenomenology in their social research.

References

1. See, e.g., Friedrich Jonas, *Geschichte der Soziologie*, vol. 2 (Reinbek bei Hamburg: Rowohlt, 1976), 169–171. It is to be noted that the common histories of sociology are oriented to Max Weber and consider Simmel a marginal thinker.
2. Leopold von Wiese, *System der Allgemeinen Soziologie als Lehre von den sozialen Prozessen und den sozialen Gebilden der Menschen (Beziehungslehre)* (München/Leipzig: Duncker & Humblot, 1933), 13, 35.
3. Ibid., 491.
4. Emile Durkheim, *Regeln der soziologischen Methode* (Neuwied/Berlin: Suhrkamp, 1961). The contrast with Simmel's unscholarly style is obvious.
5. Hermann Lotze, *Logik* (Hamburg: Felix Meiner, 1989), 550.
6. Arnold Gehlen, *Urmensch und Spätkultur* (Frankfurt: Athenäum, 1964), 24.
7. Simmel, *Soziologie. Untersuchungen über die Formen der Vergesellschaftung* (Frankfurt: Suhrkamp, 1992), 891.
8. Siegfried Kracauer, "Soziologie als Wissenschaft," in *Siegfried Kracauer, Schriften I* (Frankfurt: Suhrkamp, 1971), 65.
9. Siegfried Kracauer, *Der Detektiv-Roman: Ein philosophischer Traktat* (Frankfurt: Suhrkamp, 1979), 131, 133.
10. Margarete Susman, *Die geistige Gestalt Georg Simmels* (Tübingen: Mohr Siebeck, 1959), 28.
11. Ruth Benedict, "Configurations of Culture in North America," *American Anthropologist*, vol. 34 (1932), 24.
12. Simmel, *The Philosophy of Money* (London and New York: Routledge, 2011), 407f.
13. Simmel, *Das individuelle Gesetz—Philosophische Exkurse* (Frankfurt: Suhrkamp, 1968), 142f.
14. Simmel, *On Individuality and Social Forms*, 375.
15. Ibid., 375.
16. Ibid., 393.
17. Edmund Burnett Tylor, *Primitive Culture,* Vol. 1 (London 1871), 1. In Tyler's model of social anthropology, "culture" and "society" are used synonymously.
18. Friedrich Nietzsche, "Unzeitgemäße Betrachtungen I," *Sämtliche Werke. Kritische Studienausgabe*, Vol. 1 (München: De Gruyter, 1988), 160.
19. Paul Rock, *The Making of Symbolic Interactionism* (New York: Macmillan, 1979), 27.
20. Simmel, "A Contribution to the Sociology of Religion," *American Journal of Sociology* Vol. 3, No. 3 (1905), 361f.
21. Ibid., 368.
22. Ibid., 376.
23. Simmel, "Die Religion," *Georg Simmel: Gesamtausgabe, Band 10* (Frankfurt: Suhrkamp, 1995), 107.

Chapter 2
Forms of Sociability

2.1 Exchange Relations

The Philosophy of Money, the major work of Simmel, has been extensively commented on and discussed in sociology, less in economics. In Germany the collection of essays *Georg Simmels Philosophie des Geldes: Aufsätze und Materialien* (2003), edited by Otthein Rammstedt et al., provides a survey of the relevant topics, but it does not address the contemporary discussion about the emotional side of financial matters. To understand this point, it must be recalled that Simmel begins the Analytical Part of *The Philosophy of Money* with the sketch of a drive theory. Here, he uses the concept *Triebbefriedigung*, or "drive satisfaction," which is usually ascribed to Freud [1]. In light of this nearly psychoanalytic frame, Simmel's aim to construct a new story underneath historical materialism acquires a deeper meaning. Simmel considers the exchange of goods as the primordial form of human sociality before the later history of the rise of capitalism exposed by Karl Marx in *The Capital*.

The deeper meaning of this new story lies in Simmel's concept of personality. After the first meeting with the young German philosopher Ernst Bloch, Simmel said, "He has the Eros" (*Der hat den Eros*) [2], a statement that may be seen as proof of the validity of my original argument about Simmel's erotic way of seeing his environment. Bloch agreed with Simmel's view while studying under him. In his later turn to dialectical materialism, Bloch's judgment became a negative one. He called Simmel an impressionist writer without a philosophical core. The current interpretation of Simmel's influence on Marxist writers highlights how they distanced themselves from Simmel's image of humans. David Frisby mentions only one of Bloch's positive responses to Simmel, namely, his apercu that "there are only fifteen people in the world but these fifteen move about so quickly that we believe there to be more." It is interesting to note here that Frisby does not indicate that this passage was written in a chapter of *Das Prinzip der Hoffnung* about the inner energy that drives a person's will to power, and he does not explain the meaning of this

F. Fellmann, *Rethinking Georg Simmel's Social Philosophy*, SpringerBriefs in Sociology, https://doi.org/10.1007/978-3-030-57351-5_2

enigmatic sentence [3]. Perhaps the topic did not fit to the formal view of American sociology. In a long passage quoted by Bloch, Simmel states that the individual body is surrounded by a sort of radiation or of an aura that impresses social interaction [4]. Simmel stresses that this aura is not something mystical but is part of subjective experience. Without doubt, Simmel refers to the sexual drive in social interaction. Here, the latent erotic undercurrent of Simmel's philosophical interpretation of money becomes apparent.

Marx is known for his sharp criticism of money in *The Capital*. Simmel was obviously also aware of the negative effects of money yet he recognized "the growing spiritualization of money" [5]. Simmel sees the spirituality of money in the tendency to transform substantial value into functional value. He found that things which were too close to need were not considered valuable and things completely out of reach were also not considered valuable. The mean distance is decisive for being recognized as having worth. While all things have a determined content and therefore value, money on the contrary has its content from the value. Money symbolizes not only exchange value but also the pure idea of validity. Money is valid and nothing else. In short, the fascination of money lies in its being pure form.

Money, Simmel states, "has a very positive quality that is expressed in the negative term of lack of character" [6]. This lack of character marks the freedom that money generates. Money is only valuable if it has not yet been spent. One's being able to do with money what one likes is a necessary condition of its function. The despicableness of money, that it can take on every shape because it has no shape, leads Simmel to a surprising punch line: "It is a thing absolutely lacking in qualities and therefore cannot, as can even the most pitiful object, conceal within itself any surprises or disappointments" [7]. The young Karl Marx saw it the same way. The power of money—according to Marx—lies in that it can bring the most opposite, the most reluctant, into reciprocal touch [8]. In other words, Marx understands money as a real medium not only representing values but moving them and bringing them together. The comparison of Marx's early position with Simmel's brings to light their agreement.

In the Synthetic Part of *The Philosophy of Money* Simmel deals with human interaction according to money's circular nature; it encourages individual freedom, greater equality, and melts away hierarchic forms of patronage. This is evident in various forms of social interaction, where the opposition between "to have" and "to be" is eliminated. Simmel states that even possession is to be regarded as an action combining giving and taking. This thought could be understood as an anticipation of the current insight into the instinctual life and volatility of financial markets. The equivalence of sex and money worked out by Simmel in his analysis of prostitution sheds light on the stock exchange reacting like a prostitute.

In the last chapter, "Style of Life," Simmel's description of the metropolitan style of life has become famous. In his lecture *The Metropolis and Mental Life* (1903) Simmel references *The Philosophy of Money*:

The deepest problems of modern life flow from the attempt of the individual to maintain the independence and individuality of his existence against the sovereign powers of society, against the weight of the historical heritage and the external culture and technique of life. The antagonism represents the most modern form of the struggle which primitive man must carry on with nature for his own bodily existence. . . . Nietzsche may have seen the relentless struggle of the individual as the prerequisite for his full development, while socialism found the same thing in the suppression of all competition—but in each of these the same fundamental motive was at work, namely the resistance of the individual to being levelled, swallowed up in the social-technological mechanism [9].

The self-preservation of the individual brings human experience into permanent conflict. The inevitable conflict must not always be destructive; conflict can be constructive and gives society texture, durability, and resilience.

The metropolis or city becomes the location where the division of labor is the greatest and where individuality and individual freedom is most expanded. At the same time Simmel notes that for the individual this creates the difficulty of asserting his or her own personality within the dimensions of metropolitan life. The growth of the city, the increasing number of people in the city, and the brevity and scarcity of the inter-human contacts granted to the metropolitan human, as compared to the social intercourse of a small town, means objective culture dominates subjective culture. Modern culture in terms of language, production, art, science, etc., is at an ever-increasing distance. This is the result of increasing division of labor and the necessary specialization of individual skills. Subjective culture is, in Simmel's words, "the capacity of the actor to produce, absorb, and control the elements of objective culture. In an ideal sense, individual culture shapes, and is shaped by, objective culture." This sounds much like Marx's alienation or Weber's rationalization, which Simmel associates with the big city.

Oswald Spengler followed Simmel's view of the urban style of life in his famous book *Decline of the West* (1918/1920) [10]. Simmel read the first volume of the book before his death and gave it a positive evaluation. Spengler compares the city and the province, concepts analogous to civilization and culture, respectively. The city draws upon and collects the life of broad surrounding regions. City dwellers possess cold intelligence, a newly fashioned naturalism in their attitudes toward sex that are a return to primitive instincts, and a dying inner religiousness. The final aspect that signals the end of culture and the rise of civilization is the growth of the megalopolis, which Spengler also calls "world-city." Three or four of these world-cities will become central to global civilization: "In place of a world, there is a City, a Point, in which the whole life of broad regions is collecting while the rest dries up. In place of a type-true people, born of and grown on the soil, there is a new sort of nomad, cohering unstably in fluid masses, the parasitic city dweller, without tradition, utterly matter-of-fact, atheistic, clever, unfruitful, deeply contemptuous of the countryman."

"To the World-City," summarizes Spengler, "belongs not a folk, but a mass." The "unanchored Late Man of the Megalopolis" accosts the world with an "uncomprehending hostility to all the traditions representative of the Culture (nobility, church, privileges, dynasties, convention in art, and limits of knowledge in science)" which have preceded the civilization. The world-city dweller is pre-eminently "unfruitful," not only in the biological sense, with less children being born—but in all areas. The unfruitfulness of the population of the megalopolis is manifested "in the extinction of great art, of great courtesy, of great formal thought, of the great style in all things."

Western culture was felt to be in a crisis during the First World War. According to Spengler, the meaningful units in history are whole cultures that evolve as organisms. The final stage of each culture is "civilization," which emerges when creative impulses wane and give way to critical ones. Culture is the phase of becoming, civilization has already become. In Spengler's view, Rousseau's social contract marks the point where culture transformed itself into civilization. Spengler is convinced that Western, or European-American culture, which he calls "Faustian," is in the final state of civilization. Nevertheless, he sees in Faustian culture the highest form of human life; urban culture in particular is an inexhaustible source of creativity.

In this recognition of urban culture, Spengler agrees with Simmel's description of the urban style of life. Of course, Spengler's cyclical theory of cultural change, which uses the biological metaphor of life stages, is no longer considered valid. But this does not mean that his concept of culture itself is totally outdated. On the contrary, from the point of view of Simmel's formal sociology, culture is considered the representation of interacting elements of value. In view of globalization and the domination of international trade companies, the West will not decline, as Spengler maintained, but will change its spiritual profile and become consume-oriented, as Simmel took into consideration.

2.2   The Concept of Seduction and the Fall

Simmel's exchange theory is based on the proposition that all contacts among persons rest on the schema of giving and receiving. Social interaction as exchange has developed in the direction of objective culture; whereas the exchange of natural goods such as fruit (which rots) is limited by the period of usability, money (which does not rot) permits exchange beyond short periods of time. To explain the rise of modern forms of social exchange one can hypothesize an intermediate state between natural need and mental freedom. This intermediate state produces a form of acting that is usually called "seduction," the action of seducing or being seduced. In modern consumer societies, seduction is elaborated by "hidden persuaders" (Vance Packard).

The concept of seduction is not a central theme in Simmel's sociological writings. Only in the late version of *The Law of the Individual* (1914), where the Kantian opposition of sensation and intellect is discussed, does Simmel identify sensation with seduction as a form of acting that is essential to human existence [11]. He stresses that seduction is not something that assaults the individual from the outside but comes from within. Simmel uses the biological term "drive" to describe seduction as the stimulating side of interaction that is based on the male-female polarity.

Seduction as a form of social interaction is to be understood here in a nonmoral sense. As such, it is important to distinguish it from the legal concept. The seduction of minors is a clearly defined state of affairs that allows for no relativization. In contrast, seduction appears differently in the sexual contact between adults. When speaking about seduction as a form of guilty behavior, the bourgeois sexual morals of the nineteenth century as well as the theological concept of temptation resonates in the background. Soren Kierkegaard's existential interpretation of the role of the seducer in Mozart's *Don Giovanni* is exemplary. The seducer in the role of Don Juan is described as having angst and despair about the "dreadful nothing," which he tries to cover up with his erotic existence. This leads to the transformation of sexuality—which was bestowed to humans for reproduction—into eroticism. The superficial flight into sensual desire leaves the seducer lonely. For him, the erotic is a game with no consequences for the soul. In this attitude neither jealousy nor moral sense come into play.

However, seduction may have moral value: seduction is an operation that always involves two people. In contrast to deception, seduction is more of an attitude than an action, an attitude in which both activity and passivity are interconnected. The seducer is always the one being seduced and vice versa. Each is made to do something by the other: that which he himself cannot rationally want, but which he is emotionally inclined to do. Thus, it is not the seducer that one is unable to resist but the seduction itself. The character of seduction is to go beyond the limits; it can be a transgression not only of moral norms but also psychical and perhaps even physiological thresholds. One can say, at least, that while being seduced both wanted it, no one is willing to admit to wanting it.

If seduction is conceived as a basic form of behavior, communicative interaction becomes an ambiguous process. It cannot be clearly separated into motives and intentions; rather, the inner message often remains unstated. Consequently, seduction does not take place in the mind or body alone but in an intermediate area. In view of the Christian devaluation of sensuality, seduction is associated with sin. Simmel as a Jewish thinker points to the invention of the devil as a cowardly excuse for the ambivalent nature of humans as seduced seducers.

Once the concept of seduction has been liberated from its theological connotations and is recognized as a basic phenomenon of communication, the forms of seducing become evident. Seduction begins with signaling. In the biblical account of the Fall, the fruit from the tree of knowledge awoke the curiosity of humans. Eve is the only one to use the fruit as a sign. In the Book of Genesis, the fruit itself is not named; it is only identified as an apple in later interpretations. Although it is only vaguely stated that Eve also gave Adam some of the fruit to eat, the resulting pictorial representations portray the gesture as the offering of an apple. This gesture points to, in any case, a semiotic peculiarity like that of money as a symbolic form: the offered apple functions simultaneously as a sign-vehicle and as the relate, the object of the sign-vehicle. The paradox is that the object as a sign refers back to itself. This peculiarity confirms the erotic background of the process. The apple stands for female breasts, not the mother's breasts, and is a signal of sexual maturity.

To understand the symbolic character of the apple, a few comments on semiotics must first be made [12]. The apple lies between *icon* and *index*. *Index* is the apple not in the tree but that which is first in Eve's hand, as part of the indicating gesture. *Icon* is the apple's similarity to female breasts, which Eve was given by nature. One cannot claim that Adam was "manipulated" by Eve, for the apple was not a "hidden" persuader but an "open" one; in any case, it had unmistakable sexual overtones. In the gesture of offering, sign action and implementation collapse into each other so that one can speak about erotic communication as a fantastic presentation of the sexual act.

This statement points to the fact that their knowledge of the snake did not come from an external source but from Adam and Eve themselves. The physiological act of copulation is thus informed by knowledge and makes the association of sex and knowledge a unique kind of social formation: erotic communication. Through their emotional knowledge, Adam and Eve represent Eros in a modern way, which Simmel contrasted with Plato's interconnected theories of truth and love [13]. The certainty of erotic love is, like the knowledge of the snake, a vision. Lovers usually dream of an immortal love. This dream often proves to be an illusion, just as the snake was wrong about the promise of immortality. But the snake is not a liar, just as Eros is not. The snake perceived its promise to Eve as subjective certainty; the snake believed, just like all lovers do, in its promises.

The connection between Eros and Logos that is produced in Plato's philosophy is destroyed in the biblical account of the Fall. In Plato's theory of anamnesis, he connects both elements so that the eternal "idea of love" could be separated from the act of loving. In the Old Testament this separation is undone by means of the introduction of the snake. Knowledge of the snake has nothing to do with truth, it is carnal knowledge that is tied to the willingness to be persuaded to consume. Simmel considered consumption an inclination of humans that gave rise to money exchange; it turns the meaning of truth into a relation of subjective beliefs. Through the seduction, which is represented in theology negatively as disobedience to God, Adam and Eve became individuals. Simmel, who describes individuality as an unanalyzable unity, concludes, "[T]his individuality stands for us as the actual focal point of love, which for this very reason becomes entwined in the darkest problematic aspects of our concept of the world in contrast with the rational clarity of the platonic attitude" [14].

Humans lived innocently like animals before the Fall; like herd animals, they merely lived "next to" each other and not "with" each other. The first discussion between God and the humans occurs only *after* the seduction. God had given them instructions before the Fall, but he never communicated with them in the sense of a dialogue. Man and woman are able to become self-conscious beings only by means of erotic communication with each other and direct communication with God. This represents the advance to a new dimension of human culture and the permanent departure from animal life.

In light of the semiotic reading, we can see that the seduction can be interpreted independently of its theological meaning and as a prototype of intersubjective communication. Eros, which should have been banished by the Judeo-Christian monotheism, stops back by the semiotic "back door" once again. Through the snake's art of seduction, what holds all lovers together becomes explicit: not the partner as a seductive object but the inner drive that forms the whole person in love.

One could also regard seduction, according to Simmel, as the symbolic form of the dialectic of nearness and distance.

2.3 The Rhetoric of Seduction

The concept of seduction is in the background of Simmel's theory of coquetry and flirtation, which he situates on the playful and artistic side of interaction [15]. Simmel views flirtation as a *gestural* mode, which is to be distinguished from the explicit discursivity of love. One can conclude with Simmel that seduction is basic and becomes the art of flirtation in culture.

Flirtation has its gestures, but it has its own language as well. One would expect that Simmel, who was temporarily near to the "George Circle," where culture was considered symbolic language and art for art's sake, does consider language as an important part of culture. All the more, Simmel paralleled his method of inquiry with artistic creativity, whose standards are intrinsic to art. Furthermore, Simmel described the unity of culture as a tissue or a web, reminiscent of George's "tapestry of life." Despite these affinities, Simmel did not make the linguistic turn in philosophy during the early twentieth century. The reason for his reluctance to linguistic forms may be found in Bergson's philosophy of life, which claims that rigid concepts are not able to reproduce the flow of subjective experience.

Seduction conceived of as the archetype of intersubjectivity began in the Judeo-Christian tradition with one gesture, the offering of the forbidden fruit, but it didn't remain there. A refined allegorical code developed out of this expressive gesture, making the articulation of desire complex and communicable. A rhetoric of seduction emerges offering a unique example of the dialectic of nearness and distance that Simmel detects in social interaction.

In light of this assessment it is noteworthy that *The Theory of Communicative Action* by Jürgen Habermas makes no room for rhetoric [16]. Habermas could have formulated his theory, indeed, as part of a rhetoric. He was, however, not interested in the rhetoric approach promoted by the philosophical hermeneutics of Hans-Georg Gadamer; rather, he ascribes communication to reason giving in the sense of the logic of truth. Social life is, of course, based on the separation of private language and public arguments, but this dissolution is never entirely complete. The symbolic forms of communication influence the ways of life within a society just as economic and political institutions exert lasting influence. Public discourse and private language are therefore connected like communicating vessels.

If rhetoric is viewed as an instrument of seduction, then it has a freedom that is not at the command of the discourse of reason. Freedom, here, is not meant in the sense of metaphysical freedom of the will but as a freedom of expression that humans need in order to be able to understand each other. It is the candor character of the game of love that binds man and woman to each other. Adam and Eve are also in this respect to be seen as prototypes: they were liberated by means of the snake's rhetoric; it removed the veil from their eyes that kept them living the anonymous life in the herd.

The account of the Fall thus confirms the close connection between communication, Eros, and rhetoric in this connection.

Simmel does not explicitly deal with rhetoric but rhetoric is one aspect of philosophical culture. In the essay *"Simmel als Zeitdiagnostiker"* (postscript of *Philosophische Kultur*) Habermas claims that "Critical Theory" has overcome Simmel's concept of culture [17]. This is not completely wrong, but it should be complemented by the view of Hans Blumenberg, who, following the tracks of Simmel, spoke of an anthropological approach to rhetoric [18]. Blumenberg sees the new impact of rhetoric in the field of the use of metaphorical language. This is evident in the private language of lovers. If rhetoric can be rehabilitated at all, then only in the sign of erotic communication.

Even if rhetoric is not addressed by Simmel, the function of rhetoric is closely related to style, which is a main topic of Simmel's theory of culture. In his description of the style of modern life, Simmel mentions the rhythm and the speed of acting [19]. This, of course, is connected to the style of speaking. Here, humans can assert individual demands. In this way, style is the medium in which communication, beyond the exchange of arguments, becomes possible. This does not harm the rationality of discourses. Style does not take the place of truth but builds a framework in which competing claims of validity can be acknowledged as personal. A theory of style should be seen, accordingly, as a complement to communicative theories of truth, just as Eros must be viewed as a complement to Logos.

As Luhmann has shown, the styles of love over the course of European civilization have changed considerably [20]. Sexual life is no longer like the Eros of the Classical Ages, which was determined by an externally constructed will to form. In the Romantic period, the focus on subjective experience was predominant, but sentimental love is now gone. Love is no longer about uncontrolled devotion to feelings but requires making the internal state explicit. This is exactly where the two-sidedness of Eros, which is both anthropological radical and communicative medial, is manifested: it is an ambivalence that makes erotic love into the foundation of all forms of understanding. Style, or "attitude" as Simmel calls it, regards the person as a whole, while functional connections can be detached from personality. This is evident in Simmel's life: he was a university professor who fascinated his female audience with his erotic aura.

Love does not allow itself to be delegated, it knows no reasons, and it requires no explanation. Love has its own language of emotions. Consequently, erotic love is also a question of style. It articulates and raises into consciousness what the lovers have difficulties doing: finding their own language of emotions to express desire and pleasure in a creative manner. Thus, in Eros experience becomes a code that allows the lovers to experience an immediacy within distancing, a dialectic that is crucial in Simmel's concept of interaction. This can be in a play-form, so that the tragic style comes to an end. One plays with possibilities when one has them, and one has them when one plays with them. This does not mean that erotic love lacks seriousness but that the play-form of seriousness actually creates open forms of representation, which make its connection to other areas of life easier.

References

1. Simmel, *The Philosophy of Money*, 73: "So long as man is dominated by his impulses [literally, "is raped by his drives"] the world appears to him as an undifferentiated substance. Since it represents for him only an irrelevant means for the satisfaction of his drives ["drive-satisfaction"]—and this effect may arise from all kinds of causes—he has no interest in the nature of the objects themselves."
2. Susman, *Die geistige Gestalt Georg Simmels*, 286.
3. David Frisby, *Georg Simmel. Revised Edition* (London: Routledge, 2002), 147.
4. Ernst Bloch, *Das Prinzip Hoffnung* (Frankfurt: Surhkamp, 1959), 797.
5. Simmel, *The Philosophy of Money*, 198.
6. In chapter six of *The Philosophy of Money*, "The Style of Life," *S*immel mentions positive phenomena of modern culture and concludes that "all these are positive consequences of the negative trait of lack of character" (437).
7. Simmel, *The Philosophy of Money*, 262.
8. Karl Marx, *Economic and Philosophic Manuscripts of 1844* (Moscow: Progress Publishers, 1959), 62: "As money is not exchanged for any one specific quality, for any one specific thing, or for any particular human essential power, but for the entire objective world of man and nature, from the standpoint of its possessor it therefore serves to exchange every quality for every other, even contradictory, quality and object: it is the fraternization of impossibilities. It makes contradictions embrace." A literal translation of the last sentence is, "It forces the contradicting to kiss."
9. Simmel, *On Individuality and Social Forms*, 324.
10. Oswald Spengler, *The Decline of the West*, trans. Charles Francis Atkinson (New York: Oxford University Press, 1991).
11. See Simmel, *Kant und Goethe: Zur Geschichten der modernen Weltanschuung* (Hamburg: Tredition Classics, 2012).
12. See Charles Sanders Peirce, *Peirce on Signs: Writings on Semiotic*, ed. James Hoopes (Chapel Hill: The University of North Carolina Press, 1991).
13. See "Eros, Platonic and Modern," in *On Individuality and Social Forms*, 235–248.
14. Simmel, *On Individuality and Social Forms*, 244.
15. See Simmel, "Psychologie der Koketterie," in Otthein Ramstedt, *Georg Simmel Gesamtausgabe* (Frankfurt: Suhrkamp, 2001).
16. Jürgen Habermas, *The Theory of Communicative Action* (Cambridge: Polity Press, 1991).
17. For a critic of Habermas, see David Frisby, *Simmel and Since* (London: Routledge, 1992), 171–176.
18. Hans Blumenberg, "Anthropologische Annährung an die Aktualität der Rhetorik," in Anselm Haverkamp, *Ästhetische und metaphorologische Schriften* (Frankfurt: Suhrkamp, 2001), 406–434.
19. See "The Style of Life," in Simmel, *The Philosophy of Money*.
20. Niklas Luhmann, *Liebe als Passion. Zur Codierung der Intimität* (Frankfurt: Suhrkamp, 1994).

Chapter 3
Forms of Culturalization

3.1 The Teleological View of European Culture

In the preceding chapters, it has been shown that Simmel's principle of reciprocity, which is applied by sociologists on the horizontal level of interaction, also functions in the vertical direction as well. According to the program of genetic phenomenology, reciprocity works bottom up and top down within a single culture. In this chapter, it will be shown that reciprocity applies to the relations between different cultures that are closely related. Europe and America provide the most succinct example of this process. Here, too, the qualitative view makes clear that sexual life is the basic level of human culture, underlying other levels of *vita activa* such as working or marketing.

Simmel writes in a prominent passage, "Culture is the way from a closed unity through unfolded plurality to unfolded unity" [1]. It is obvious that Simmel in this oft-quoted passage interprets culture teleologically according to the zeitgeist of his time. The European spirit was deeply permeated by idealistic philosophy and the primacy of reason in the sense of logos. Ancient Greek philosophy used the term in different ways. Modern thinking understands logos as the rational of an argument in opposition to an intuition or irrational inspiration. The primacy of pure reason has been criticized as "logocentrism." Since Simmel's concept of culture is based on the interaction of objective and subjective culture, he transcends the logocentric perspective.

To understand logos in the broader sense of the term, Simmel can be considered the precursor of Ernst Cassirer, who among Neo-Kantians was the only one to take into consideration the intertwining of Logos and Eros in his reconstruction of Plato's philosophy. Cassirer interprets Plato's understanding of Eros as the result of the exciting interaction between body and soul. He writes, "The Eros of the soul is the deepest and most immediate revelation of the dialectical character of empirical reality" [2]. Cassirer claims that the dialectic that Plato had in mind involves a "synergistic" exchange in which a shared foundation of understanding is sought:

F. Fellmann, *Rethinking Georg Simmel's Social Philosophy*, SpringerBriefs in Sociology, https://doi.org/10.1007/978-3-030-57351-5_3

"Eros is the Logos of the soul," in Cassirer's words [3]. This does not mean that Eros is the dark side of Logos; rather, Eros is the clarification of desire through intimate relationships, which only lovers can have with each other.

Many aspects of Simmel's cultural philosophy, e.g., "erotic logos," can be compared to Edmund Husserl. Simmel and Husserl had met and were good acquaintances. Although their ways of reasoning were different, Husserl was analytical and Simmel intuitive, they were akin on an emotional level. They were both fascinated by the charm of the Italian life-world [4]. Simmel was not only a philosopher of European culture, he lived it. All the more, his faith in European culture was shaken by the hatred of German chauvinist intellectuals during the First War. Twenty years later, Husserl was subject to a similar fate. In his lecture of 1935 entitled "*Die Krisis des europäischen Menschentums und die Philosophie*" ("Philosophy and the Crisis of European Man") [5] he considers the idea of the "good European" and tries to define a balanced relation to other cultures. Husserl agrees that every culture has its own right to exist, but he is convinced that Europe, through Greek *logos*, will always endeavor to make other cultures European, and that this endeavor is mentally justified. How Husserl defends his position can be found in a few passages of his lecture:

> 'The spiritual image of Europe'—what is it? It is exhibiting the philosophical idea immanent in the history of Europe (of spiritual Europe). To put it another way, it is its immanent teleology, which, if we consider mankind in general, manifests itself as a new human epoch emerging and beginning to grow, the epoch of a humanity that from now on will and can live only in the free fashioning of its being and its historical life out of rational ideas and infinite tasks [6].

This statement makes clear that the idea of Europe derives from intentional consciousness as a goal in itself, as an "immanent teleology," as Husserl calls it. It is located in a geographical space or in a particular unit of time in terms of coexistence or succession, it has its own history. About the nation-states of Europe, Husserl states:

> No matter how inimical the European nations may be toward each other, still they have a special inner affinity of spirit that permeates all of them and transcends their national differences. It is a sort of fraternal relationship that gives us the consciousness of being at home in this circle. This becomes immediately evident as soon as, for example, we penetrate sympathetically into the historical process of India, with its many peoples and cultural forms. In this circle there is again the unity of a family-like relationship, but one that is strange to us. On the other hand, Indians find us strangers and find only in each other their fellows [7].

Husserl recognizes that every culture perceives other cultures as strangers and that every culture is convinced of its own uniqueness. But from a philosophical viewpoint, this historical description needs a higher level of epistemic justification. To arrive at this higher level of justification, Husserl continues:

> We get a hint of that right in our own Europe. Therein lies something unique, which all other human groups, too, feel with regard to us, something that apart from all considerations of expediency, becomes a motivation for them—despite their determination to retain their spiritual autonomy—constantly to Europeanize themselves, whereas we, if we understand ourselves properly, will never, for example, Indianize ourselves. I mean we feel (and with all

its vagueness this feeling is correct) that in our European humanity there is an innate entelechy that thoroughly controls the changes in the European image and gives to it the sense of a development in the direction of an ideal image of life and of being, as moving toward an eternal pole [8].

Husserl locates the uniqueness and the superiority of the European mind in the spiritual kingdom of Platonic ideas. This permits Husserl to assert that people of other cultures also feel attracted to the European mind. Movement toward an "eternal pole," as Husserl calls it, is not utopic fiction; it is the search for meaning and truth that unites all rational beings. The current "mental globalization" confirms Husserl's way of seeing, but with the important modification that communication takes place on a more basic level of common subjective experience.

When compared to Simmel, it becomes clear that Husserl as the author of *Logical Investigations* understands the development of logos in a purely rationalistic sense. Simmel states, to the contrary, in his late essay *Die Wendung zur Idee*, which can be translated as *The Shift Toward Idea*, that cultural progress is based on the creativity of life. This means that life is mainly concerned with significance in the sense of emotional intelligence. Simmel's concept of life is not only valid for personal life but for entire cultures.

As circumstances and problems change, and as issues are driven back to their basic presuppositions, philosophers are forced to reflect on culture's proper meaning. For Husserl, the meaning of culture is always directed to truth as the definite end. Truth without reality, though, remains an abstract concept, one that must be filled with concrete experiences. With this modification, Husserl's teleological idea of Europe corresponds to Simmel's view of cultural evolution, which tends to fragmentation and is permeated by conflict. This leads to a current problem, one that gives European intellectuals much to contemplate: confrontation with the new self-confidence of the Americans. Europe first or America first? The answer that Simmel would have given is nowadays particularly up-to-date.

3.2 The Idea of Europe Versus the Meaning of America

The concept of Americanism (*Amerikanismus* or *Amerikanisierung*) became popular in Germany in the early twentieth century. It had a negative connotation given Nietzsche's view of the American people: stupid moneymakers without cultural formation. Simmel, too, understood America in this way, identifying mechanization with Americanization. Nevertheless, there was also a cultural current that identified America as the land of the free since its Constitution was founded on democratic equality, whereas the German Constitution was founded on inequality.

Longing for freedom is the motif of Franz Kafka's novel *America*, written between 1911 and 1914, published posthumously. Only the first chapter of this novel, "The Stoker", appeared separately in 1913. The story describes the wanderings of 16-year-old German immigrant Karl, who was forced to go to New York City to escape the scandal of his seduction by a housemaid. As the ship arrives in the

United States, he becomes friends with a stoker and has bizarre experiences of personal alienation in the land of limitless possibilities. At the end of the book, Karl gets engaged at the "Nature Theatre of Oklahoma," where he is welcomed by the vastness of the valleys and adopts the name "Negro" as his own.

In some sense Simmel, who had also never visited the United States, may have shared Kafka's ambivalent view of America. In letters from 1918, Simmel juxtaposes European culture and the American way of life; he complains about the "suicide" of Europe, which, as a result of WWI, was no longer the humanistic role model for the civilized world. In view of the decline of Europe, Simmel finds that an American global culture, combining utilitarian pragmatism with humanistic ideals, could eventually have primacy over Europe [9].

In view of Simmel's unique supranational perspective, it is interesting to examine how the concept of Europe has been discussed since WWI. A strong anti-Americanism existed among German intellectuals. Sigmund Freud in *Civilization and Its Discontents* (1930) reflected on the nature of culture and discovered a grave danger in what he calls "the psychological misery of the masses," which is reminiscent of David Riesman's *The Lonely Crowd* (1950).

> Freud concludes, "This danger is most threatening where the bonds of a society are chiefly constituted by the identification of its members with one another, while individuals of the leader type do not acquire the importance that should fall to them in the formation of a group. The present cultural state of America would give us a good opportunity for studying the damage to civilization which is thus to be feared. But I shall avoid the temptation of entering upon a critique of American civilization; I do not wish to give an impression of wanting myself to employ American methods" [10].

For Freud, America represented a materialistic and prudish culture yet was also immensely seductive, alluring, almost irresistible. In opposition to crude anti-Americanism, this ambivalent attitude is characteristic of more sensible thinkers. It is expressed in the famous novel *Manhattan Transfer* (1925) by John Dos Passos. He attacks the monetary indifference of metropolitan life, portraying Manhattan as merciless yet teeming with energy and creativity. In this fashion, Henry Miller in *Tropic of Capricorn* (1939/1961) compared modernization in Europe and America. On the one hand, he complains that in America the destruction is complete and all historical traces have been destroyed. On the other, he is impressed by the power of erotic life on Broadway [11]. This sounds like an echo of Freud's dialectical theory of culture as the realm of antagonistic forces, Eros and Thanatos. It also reminds us of Simmel's dialectical view of cultural life as permeated by irreconcilable conflicts.

The widespread European anti-Americanism was also reflected in the fact that many American writers and intellectuals lived in Paris in the 1920s, which they viewed as the paradise of continental culture with the salon of Gertrude Stein at the center. In a later edition of Ernest Hemingway's *A Movable Feast* (1936), one can read what he once told a friend, "If you are lucky enough to have lived in Paris as a young man, then wherever you go for the rest of your life, it stays with you, for Paris is a moveable feast." "An American in Paris"—the title of Gershwin's musical—was also a topic for German thinkers in the Weimar Republic, namely, for Walter Benjamin and Siegfried Kracauer.

The primacy of European culture led intellectuals to the opinion that America has no culture at all. This prejudice overlooks how Americans originally came from Europe and brought their culture with them. Here, the bottom up direction of cultural evolution is turned upside down. The alleged lack of culture is the result of an adaptive transformation of older elements into a new way of life. This process corresponds to Arnold Gehlen's 1964 book *Urmensch und Spätkultur* (*Primitive Man and Late Culture*). Gehlen shows how elements of a late culture are the foundation of a new and sound culture. The principle of cultural reciprocity regards the forms of action. Gehlen distinguishes between three forms of action, each of which corresponds to a worldview: practical, representational, and idealistic. All three forms are interlinked in the American way of life, a consequence of its heterogeneous origins.

American culture was welcomed in Germany after WWII; besides the Marshall Plan there was the democratic denazification and reeducation program. Visiting American universities (Harvard, Yale, etc.) became the highlight of the careers of German academics. But this changed in 2000, as American culture is nowadays seen more realistically, if not slightly pejoratively. This change in attitude toward American culture is evident in the works *Foreign Country America* (2016) and *Other Country* (2018) by the popular German journalist Ingo Zamperoni [12].

3.3 The Making of America

Whereas Europe is the outcome of a long historical process, America is considered to have been built by immigrants. In the famous book *We Who Made America* (1931) Carl Wittke provided a comprehensive view of all immigrant groups and what they have contributed to American culture. A prominent group was the Jewish immigrants at the end of the nineteenth century, who brought with them a strong dedication to ideals. This issue was apparently religious and against Islam. The Jewish journalist Abraham Cahan described the Jewish immigrant's process of Americanization a 100 years ago [13]. He delineates the clash of cultures and shows the dilemmas of acculturation. In his story *The Imported Bridegroom* the clash between religious faith and secularism is obvious, and the question remains whether this still works today and whether it is a real threat to the pluralism characteristic of American pragmatism.

Studies about immigrants refer in a general way to Simmel's essay on the stranger, which can be regarded as prototypical of immigrants. By connecting Simmel's analysis of the stranger to his concept of social distance, we can better understand the properties of immigrant communities, their internal organization, and their relation to society as a whole [14]. Immigrant communities are, to be sure, broadening horizons; at the same time, they bring about dissolution of the homogenous community rooted in a homeland. This ambivalence prevents the modern world from being either a clash of cultures or a golden mixture of cultures. It is, instead, an interaction of different positions, a social exchange that benefits all parties even in the very confrontation of their different lifestyles. In globalization, the demand for new forms of individual self-expression and self-validation is growing and legitimate. On the other hand, individualism has to be compatible with the tenets of social belief and tradition in the different nation-states.

Irrespective of the immigration topic, the fabric of America has been recorded by Gertrude Stein. The title of her early novel *The Making of Americans* (1925) suggests a wide panorama of American ways of life, but instead tells the story of a family's progress over three generations, radically reworking the traditional family to encompass her vision of personality and psychological relationships. The focus of the story is a girl about to get married. Through this familiar lens, Stein molds the ideal image of an American woman, who dreams of becoming a wife and a mother, of having her own family. Thus, the making of the family and the making of America are structurally consistent. The cultural differences are revealed in erotic behavior. If one looks at India, where sex and religion are closely connected, marriage is socially arranged. In Europe love is general, but there are differences in courtship between northern and southern countries. The "Italian lover" has been and is still the dream of bourgeois women. Even Henry Miller's Mona, the taxi girl, is not sophisticated, she is a Vulcan of power. And the American adaption of Fanny Hill by Erica Jong does not get into the inner life of a European prostitute. In this way, the making of America is the opposite to Simmel's making of European culture. Consequently, American sociology does not have an intimate relationship with Simmel's view of life. This difference is not only to be considered negatively as a lack; in these different cultural mentalities, Eros turns out to be the source of the greatest richness in modern feelings of life.

Over time, conventional family structure has undergone influential changes, including divorce and the introduction of single-parent families, unwed mothers, and same-sex marriage. Social movements such as feminism or stay-at-home fathers have contributed to the creation of alternative family forms, generating the transition from the family to sex and intimacy. Anthony Giddens, whose sociological thinking was committed to Simmel, suggests that the disengagement of sex from procreation has paved the way to plastic sexuality in modern intimate relationships [15]. Despite apparent social changes, the traditional family structure is still valid, mentally speaking. This confirms Simmel's analysis of the double role of the family, which functions as a medium of individualization and of collectivization [16]. Simmel considers the family a synthetic unity, a whole uniting heterogeneous personalities. His study of groups hypothesized the existence of dyads and triads: A dyad is a group of two people that interact, and a triad is another person added to create more communicational interactions. This has been called a "Simmelian tie," a concept used in the analysis of modern social organizations [17].

Simmel considers the family to be the emotional nucleus of society. Despite his high regard for the nuclear family, which he viewed as the emotional tie of society, Simmel carried on intimate relations with his lifelong mistress. This shows that Eros functions on different levels, private and public, which interact. This double point of view was analyzed by Talcott Parsons in the 1950s and is evident in America today [18]. Since Donald Trump became President of the USA, the question of values in politics has entered discussion. Trump has divorced twice and married three times. Several of his longtime friends have been charged with soliciting prostitution. Yet he promotes the family as central to his own life and to the cohesion of American society. Regardless of political positions, his slogan "America first" sheds light on purpose and value in the process of democratization of social institutions.

"America first" refers mainly to national security. The terrorist attacks of 9/11 have led to the conviction that America, the haven of freedom and justice, is now the target of evil as such. Trump has put many Islamic states under general suspicion. This promotes dualisms that divide the world into "good" and "evil". The origin of this worldview is of religious nature and belongs to Manichaeism, which has nothing in common with the specific dualisms inherent in the social forms that Simmel analyzed. Manichaean thinking was thought to be definitively overcome by the Enlightenment. Unfortunately, the dialectics of Enlightenment teach us that Manicheism can never be overcome completely. This is the real mental catastrophe caused by terrorist attacks.

Another aspect of the declared primacy of the USA concerns the economy. Trump as a businessman embodies this ideology in the form of welfare, a pragmatic mixture of religious faith and capitalism. This reminds us of Max Weber, who is best known for his thesis combining economic sociology and sociology of religion, which is elaborated in the book *The Protestant Ethic and the Spirit of Capitalism*. Weber argues that "it was in the basic tenets of Protestantism to boost capitalism" [19]. Echoing this passage, Trump declared the USA was no longer willing to pay for European countries exploiting the United States economically.

It pays to think about what Trump has said about trade in light of Simmel's concept of economic exchange in *The Philosophy of Money*. Simmel esteems exchange as a creative process and as the primary source of value. Value formation provides the cultural foundation of society:

> Herein probably lies the ultimate motive for the several forms, the legal guaranties, the various public and traditional assurance which lend support to commerce in all early cultures … An analogy to this would be provided by … the sale and exchange of women. The radically new form of marriage introduced thereby is thus immediately set in a way that structures the choice of individuals [20].

The structure and function of exchange in late modern societies show that Trump as a born businessman is not completely wrong to connect price and moral value [21].

Most interesting from the sociological point of view is cultural identity and public appearance. Trump is perceived in Europe as a braggart and boaster. His appearance may be compared to *The Ugly American* (1958) in the political novel by Eugene Burdick and William Lederer. The title of the novel is a play on Graham Greene's novel *The Quiet American* (1955). John F. Kennedy was so impressed with the book that he sent a copy to each of his colleagues in the United States Senate. The term "ugly American" came to be used to refer to the "loud and ostentatious" American politicians. Sixty years later, the book has become, with the presidency of Trump, an authentic description of the American abroad.

On the other hand, American culture is "primitive" in a positive sense. The hard line of American conservatives may be regarded as a genuine reaction to the arrogance of European intellectuals who were influenced by the German idealism of the nineteenth century, just as Simmel was. The strong emphasis on solidarity and empathetic understanding by German thinkers differs from sociologists, who focus on social difference and economic success.

Concerning appearance, one may ask if Trump is an "adventurer." Simmel depicts the adventurer as a restless, tireless hiker. This seems to be the case with Trump, who is estimated to be erratic, unpredictable. But one must not forget that the adventurer is a player, and Trump, too, is one. When asked about the meaning of his meeting with the North Korean despot Kim in 2018, Trump said, "Everybody plays games." This corresponds to Simmel's concept of the archetypal play-form of all human sociality, which has been elaborated by Erving Goffman in his book *The Presentation of Self in Everyday Life* (1959).

To sum up, "America first" refers to a new American evaluation of culture that represents experiences closer to empirical evidence and differs in some way from common transatlantic values. Here, a new clash of culture within the West becomes possible. This is not surprising in view of Simmel's concept of culture, which confirms the eternal law of conflict in human ways of social life. But this does not automatically entail the decline of the West. On the contrary, conflict within and between cultures can be constructive. The different worlds of culture are not completely antagonistic, they conflict only insofar as they compete for social resources. Of particular interest are the valuable resources for improving one's chances of being acknowledged as someone who is important. In contemporary America, the subject matter of sociology extends to every situation involving human interaction where exchange, domination, success, immigration, etc., are considered socially important. Many of Simmel's properties of cultural forms can be identified in this new trend, which is evident in the studies on Simmel's relational sociology. But Simmel's social philosophy broadens the horizon by explaining the advancement of human culture as a circular process of real and ideal exchange. This may be a way to avoid the clash of culture that has since become an urgent problem. Simmel's genetic phenomenology of the process of differentiation provides useful suggestions for how to preserve the one world that we now live in despite the plurality of that world's cultural traditions.

References

1. Simmel, "Der Begriff und die Tragödie der Kultur," *Das Individuelle Gesetz* (Frankfurt: Suhrkamp, 1968), 118.
2. Ernst Cassirer, "Die Philosophie der Griechen," in Max Dessoir, *Die Geschichte der Philosophie* (Wiesbaden: Fourier, 1927), 88.
3. Ibid.
4. See Simmel's letter to Husserl in *Buch des Dankes an Georg Simmel*, 85.

5. Edmund Husserl, *Phenomenology and the Crisis of Philosophy*, trans. Quentin Lauer (London: Harper Torchbooks, 1965).
6. Ibid., 156.
7. Ibid., 157.
8. Ibid., 158.
9. See Simmel's letters to Hermann Keyserling in *Das Individuelle Gesetz*: "One could be supra-national to a degree, that, if an American world-culture is emerging ... there is no reason for complaint. Why should Europe have the primacy of culture forever?" (245).
10. Sigmund Freud, *Civilization and Its Discontents*, trans. J. Strachey (New York: W.W. Norton & Company, 1961), 75.
11. Henry Miller, *Tropic of Capricorn* (New York: Grove Press, 1961), 217.
12. Ingo Zamperoni, *Fremdes Land Amerika* (Frankfurt: Ullstein, 2016); Ingo Zamperoni, *Anderland* (Frankfurt: Ullstein, 2018).
13. Abraham Cahan, *Yekl and The Imported Bridegroom and Other Stories* (New York: Dover Publications, 1970).
14. Donald N. Levine, Ellwood B. Carter, Eleanor Miller Gorman, "Simmel's Influence on American Sociology," *American Journal of Sociology* Vol. 81, No. 4 (1976).
15. Anthony Giddens, *The Transformation of Intimacy: Sexuality, Love, and Eroticism in Modern Societies* (Cambridge: Polity Press, 1992).
16. See Kurt H. Wolff, *The Sociology of Georg Simmel* (Illinois: The Free Press, 1950).
17. See "Simmelian Tie," *Wikipedia*, last modified January 26, 2018, https://en.wikipedia.org/wiki/Simmelian_tie
18. "The Incest Taboo in Relation to Social Structure and the Socialization of the Child," *British Journal of Sociology*, 1954, V, 101–117.
19. See McKinnon, "Elective Affinities of the Protestant Ethic: Weber and the Chemistry of Capitalism," *Sociological Theory* 28 (1), 108–126.
20. Simmel, *On Individuality and Social Forms*, 67. See Simmel, *The Philosophy of Money*, 105.
21. See Simmel about the analogy between money and intellectuality, both of which are elements of objective culture, and about an all-out trade war between the major economies and allies: "The intensity of modern economic conflicts in which no mercy is shown is only an apparent counter-instance of such features of the money economy since these conflicts are unleashed by direct interest in money itself. For it is not only that they take place in an objective sphere in which the importance of the person lies not only in his character but also in his embodiment of a particular objective economic potential, and where the deadly antagonistic competitor of today is the cartel ally of tomorrow. Rather, what is of primary importance is that the rules established within one sphere may be totally different from those considered valid outside that sphere but which are none the less influenced by them" (*The Philosophy of Money*, 470).

Chapter 4
Intimate Relations

4.1 Sociology of Sex

The former chapter dealt with the high level of patterns of culture; we will now take a step down in this chapter to the basis of all levels of existence. The higher forms of sociation are widely discussed. In American sociology, Simmel is present especially through the mediation of Robert Ezra Park, who specified that the leading idea of sociology was to describe forms of social interaction, including the function of these forms. Generally speaking, erotic interaction is not in the focus of Simmel's reception, neither in Germany nor in America. In view of Simmel's assertion in his essay on flirtation that "the relationship between the sexes provides the prototype for countless relationships between the individual and the interindividual life," [1] it is surprising that this central relationship in social life has remained largely neglected by sociologists. An exception to be noted is a work by Murray S. Davis, *Intimate Relations* (1973). Following Simmel's phenomenological method, Davis analyzes the psychological factors by which intimacy evolves. He examines Simmel's "digression about the sociology of the senses," which explains the effects of "reciprocal perception" and provides clues for a relevant research program that still needs to be carried out in order to confirm that intimate relations are mainly sensory and emotional [2]. In erotic love, partners unconsciously lose their former selves in each other by creating each other anew. This dialectical paradigm of love does not follow strict, objective rules. Instead, intimates are motivated and held together by the ideal and sometimes fantastic construction of their relationship.

French sociologists consider social cohesion to be a serious problem in Simmel's theory of relations [3]. According to them, Emile Durkheim is better at connecting the problems of cohesion and of relation. There are many forms of cohesion, for example, food presentation, the gift, and others. Although social cohesion is not a dominant topic in Simmel's work, his description of genetic schemes of interaction covers the cohesive force that is not outside the relation but its immanent form. This is especially true for intimate relations that connect the partners even after a divorce.

F. Fellmann, *Rethinking Georg Simmel's Social Philosophy*, SpringerBriefs in Sociology, https://doi.org/10.1007/978-3-030-57351-5_4

Thus, a sociology of intimacy such as Simmel was attempting can do without the French spirit.

Simmel attempted to show that loving relations are constituted non-verbally and immediately, primarily through the sense of sight. Sartre's famous analysis of "the look" can be read as a confirmation of the social effect of eye contact. According to Simmel, the look from eye to eye is the primordial form of subjective reciprocity, it generates an emotional bond that is stronger and more durable than objective knowledge about the partner. In an adaption of Simmel's formulation, the looking eye that strives to unveil the soul of the other unveils the soul of the looking one [4]. Eye-to-eye contact becomes the tender look characteristic of lovers—"Here's looking at you, kid" is the assertion of Rick in *Casablanca*.

It should be noted that Simmel's sociological view of the senses, especially of sight, does not correspond to Freud's view, which derives all social relations from sexuality. In his discussion of incest and the ban on marriage between relatives, Simmel stresses that cultures develop social forms to master sexuality, which is volatile and does not result in reliable bonds. In contrast, erotic love becomes a spiritual adhesive for a loving couple. Using a metaphorical expression, one could say that lovers as sensual beings are all made of glue. Thus, Simmel's perspective of erotic cohesion provides a fundamental element for building a sociology through relation.

Among Simmel's papers about erotic love translated in English, *Flirtation* is the most typical of Simmel's style [5]. The posthumously published fragment *On Love* is part of Simmel's foray into a philosophy of emotional life that points toward later attempts by the phenomenologist Max Scheler to study basic human emotions. In *The Problem of the Sexes* Simmel reflects on the psychology of women and reveals many typical male attitudes toward women. Finally, *Female Culture* reflects Simmel's interest in the women's movement in Germany; it is also an application of his theory of alienation in objective culture. It bears directly on some issues in the current women's movement [6].

Simmel's views about erotic love and female culture are mentioned in several articles in the classical *Handwörterbuch der Sexualwissenschaft,* edited in 1922 by Max Marcuse [7]. In any case, Simmel is one of the founders of the modern sociology of sex [8]. In *Sociology: Inquiries into the Construction of Social Forms* Simmel writes that sexuality, which is the general and the impersonal factor serving the survival of the species, is experienced by humans as the most intimate and personal [9]. "Sexual intercourse as synthesis of the personal and the general"— according to the formula in the "table of contents"—forms the psychological secrecy of human sexuality [10].

The answer to the question, why do people experience sexuality as intimacy, is a complex one. Sexuality is a biological need that humans share with animals. But there is a difference. Animals copulate in public and lack intimacy. Humans, to the contrary, feel shame, which indicates that human sexuality has passed beyond the act of procreation and has become a source of self-consciousness. The step from sexuality to eroticism is a way of becoming aware of living with all the senses in the social world. This step is crucial for understanding Simmel's generative view of social life, which is made up of strata beginning with the germline and ending in self-consciousness.

Simmel states that entering into an intimate relationship is connected with sexuality, and that for most people sexual love represents the total personality. On the other side, the preponderance of the erotic bond may suppress the potentials of the individual lying outside the erotic sphere [11]. This demonstrates that in sexual life nature and culture are entangled in a dialectical way that makes the mating mind unique. Although Simmel knows that the sexual need is inborn and genetic, he stresses the important role of eroticism in culture and personality in view of the malleability of human nature. And he did not overlook the conflictual nature of intimate relations. Among the innumerable conflicts is the repression of sexuality, a central topic of Freud's theory of the influence of sexuality on the human mind.

The interrelation of sex and repression is confirmed by different areas of anthropological research. Ethnology has shown that the sexual drive is a natural force active in all areas of culture. Bronislaw Malinowski, although disagreeing with Freud's treatment of the sex impulse, acknowledges that psychoanalysis has paved the way to a dynamic theory of the human mind and its unconscious sides [12]. Modern sociobiology considers Darwinian sexual selection as only one factor in the evolution of sociability. Edward O. Wilson has demonstrated how the antagonism between sex and sociality, mostly displayed by animals, is mitigated in human society by the cultural forms of courtship [13]. Culture transforms the biological imperative of the sexual drive into the eroticism characteristic of intimate relations [14]. Eroticism, unlike mere sexual intercourse, is a psychological issue dependent on, yet independent of, sexuality. Liberation from sexual need, or better its erotic sublimation, opens the door to human individuation and free will. Though sexuality and eroticism are two essentially opposite categories of human life, Simmel considers the step from sexuality to eroticism a gradual process of epigenesis that is disconnected from cultural teleology [15].

In light of Simmel's life-form antithesis, the erotic is a cultural form that makes sexuality a complex experience. On the one hand, erotic love disturbs social cooperation, and, on the other, Eros equals creativity, as it stimulates the imagination in delicate situations. Unlike animals, humans do not have sex with some member of their species; they make love to a special individual. The dilemma of how to make peace among sexual competitors is solved with the establishment of the family. The nuclear family is the key to the high level of cooperation that distinguishes human societies. Humans separate the sexual and the social in a dialectic of nearness and distance. Though most people have personalized sex, in modern consumer societies sexual performances tend to run away and to become fixed rituals, as was the case in courtly cultures of the past. Strangely enough, as a result of modern individualism, lovers act according to the principle of imitation like puppets on the string of social fashions.

Fashion, as Simmel has shown, "as a universal phenomenon in the history of our race," is experienced as being on the side of creative activity yet one feels protected by the mainstream of collective behavior. This also applies to erotic experience. In fashionable imitation Eros loses much of its emotional intensity and leaves behind the deeper meaning of passionate love. Simmel states, "there is good reason why externals—clothing, social conduct, amusements—constitute the specific field of fashion, for here no dependence is placed on really vital motives of human actions" [16]. This independence of drives is linguistically expressed in the current saying "to have fun" as a common motive of social actions like hiking and parties. Post-modern lovers strive to synthesize the vital and the formal, the subjective and the objective principle of their relation. To accomplish such a compromise, a new art of living is needed that redeems vital emotionality in the distant and cool relations prevailing at the present time. Simmel considers it a sociological task of the art of living to convert distance into a relationship of nearness [17]. To fulfill this task, Simmel's analysis of the senses affords interesting elements for contemporary concerns about the intimate relations between men and women.

4.2 Eroticism Still Matters

The gap between subjective and objective culture conceived by Simmel in *The Philosophy of Money* (1900) became more pressing a decade later. In the essay "The Conception and the Tragedy of Culture" (1911) he states that culture is moving in an ineluctable tension between life and form and never becomes a unity resting in itself [18]. The tragedy results from antagonisms, and human catastrophes are no accidental slips. Here Simmel may have felt the rise of WWI. Nevertheless, Simmel does not indulge himself in cultural pessimism as Spengler did. In his essay of 1914 "The Conflict in Modern Culture" Simmel sounds more optimistic in stating that the new aspect of his time is the fact that life is rebelling against form as such, a situation that is absolutely new in the European history of culture.

At the end of his essay Simmel deals with sexual relationships. This seems to be marginal but it points to the erotic undercurrent of Simmel's concept of culture. Simmel states that the life-form dualism is expanded in sexual life as practiced by the new generation. In modern times the dynamic of sensuality has become so powerful that it not only modifies its forms and creates new ones but also strives to get rid of every form. This, according to Simmel, does not function in the long run, because it is a self-contradiction and would lead to arbitrariness and emptiness without firm support, which is necessary for culture to survive. Consequently, modern eroticism seems to lead to promiscuity and anarchic lust.

Upon consideration, though, it becomes clear that modern forms of erotic practices overcome sensual alienation and pursue sexuality more concretely: "Genuine erotic life in fact flows naturally in individual channels. Opposition is directed against forms because they force it into generalized schemata and thereby overpower its uniqueness. The struggle between life and form is fought here less abstractly and less metaphysically as a struggle between individuality and generalization" [19]. This is a characteristic turn of Simmel's endeavor to make general concepts more concrete. Subjective experience entails desire's dissonance and is apt to embrace conceptual fluidity and relativity. Simmel does not rate the uprising of informal life critically as a loss of substance but finds it to be forward-looking, as a possible springboard for a new relation between life and form on a higher level of reflection. What Simmel has in mind is a flexibilization of the form, through which modern man or, as Simmel formulates, the soul is on the way to itself. This becomes evident in the mobility of modern people, who are no longer bound to their native soil as the origin of culture. This creates a new individualism whose contribution to social differentiation has been analyzed in detail by Simmel [20]. Looking up from here to *The Risk Society* of Ulrich Beck, one becomes aware that the way into "another modernity" was already mapped out by Simmel [21]. The dynamic of individualization has liberated modern man from cultures structured by classes. This is felt, not least, in the relationship of the sexes, which leads to a new arrangement of the roles of males and females. In their brilliant study *The Normal Chaos of Love* (1990), Ulrich Beck and Elisabeth Beck-Gernsheim argue that the nature of *love* in modern society is changing completely and creating opportunities for new forms of social interaction, such as those Simmel developed in *Law of the Individual*.

It is noteworthy that Simmel, probably impressed by the life-reform movement of his time, evaluates liberation from traditional gender roles positively. What cultural sociology later described as a characteristic of the "fun society" (*Spaßgesellschaft*), namely, the emotional setting of social relations in the spontaneous emergence of groups, applies to erotic lifestyle. Personal experience is regarded as a personal corrective of the power of rigid social structures and institutions like marriage. In this sense Simmel understands the criticism of traditional sexual relations as the expression of a "new ethics" that is open to changing gender roles.

Although Simmel considers erotic life basic to the growth of a new ethics, he does not subscribe to Freud's libidinal theory. Freud considered the formative experiences of personality to be of a principally somatic nature centered on infantile sexuality, whereas Simmel holds on to the interactionist view in intimate relations between adults. For him the basic characteristic of all interpersonal behavior is reciprocity. The first realization of equal reciprocity is the two-person group, the loving couple, normally legalized in marriage. In modern culture, with its free sexual relationships in broader groups, eroticism produces permanent conflicts between vital needs and moral ideals. Conflict is unavoidable and sometimes destructive, if not tragic, but is also the source of mental creativity. The conflicts inherent in erotic love in particular are constructive; they bring about unexpected forms of living together and can thus be considered the royal road to cultural diversity.

Simmel's evaluation of erotic love was revolutionary in his time because it laid bare the unofficial and unacknowledged side of human life. More important is the fact that erotic love is not one of the many facets of society Simmel is dealing with—group, role, domination, subordination, conflict, exchange, reciprocity, and so on; it is rather the until now overlooked psychological stratum of modern societies. The essayistic way of argumentation, complained of by more systematic or empirically oriented sociologists, can be understood as an indirect confirmation of the pervasive presence of eroticism in modern life, especially in urban life, given that much of Simmel's career was spent in Berlin at a time when that city was at the forefront of modernist risk society. In the encounters of many different people, unexpected combinations and confusions arise; but there is an inherent drive to solve problems in an unexpected way. This has become the dominant characteristic of modern life and forms of love, which are directed to the future rather than to the past. This is Simmel's more optimistic view of modernity, where conflicts turn out to be constructive and set free creativity in both private and public social life.

4.3   Sex Differences

Nobody really denies the existence of biological and cultural differences between the sexes in erotic behavior. Although Simmel was primarily concerned with the ways in which culture builds personality, he did not overlook the biological impact of the sexual drive. After WWII, the German sociologist Helmut Schelsky in his classic study *Soziologie der Sexualität* (1955) championed the view that culture, not nature, is the primary force in shaping individual personality. In agreement with Margaret Mead, Schelsky asserts that ethnological material shows that most features generally called "male" and "female" stem from biological sex differences. On the other hand, he warns sociologists against the other tendency, to exaggerate and take as absolute the formal structures of social lives. He claims that forms of sociation are meaningful answers to the biological nature of humans.

From the psychobiological point of view, humans, a species with only moderate sex differences in structure, exhibit profound sex differences in the mind or psyche. In our century, sex differences tend to be overlooked by scholars for fear of being labeled conservative. Nevertheless, sex differences are still at work. The traditional belief that female intelligence is associated with pronounced feelings bound to subjective experiences is confirmed by emotional intelligence research. To use the words of John Stuart Mill, "a woman seldom runs wild after an abstraction." Men, on the contrary, are usually passionate about abstract thought, and consequently male intelligence functions with less emotional restraint. These basic sex differences in the mind have been mentioned by research in evolutionary psychology.

Sociology began to focus on cooperation at the end of the twentieth century. Success through collective work and cooperation has been called "social capital." Communitarian theory of social capital, mostly inspired by Robert Putnam [22], says that women can achieve any aim if they work collectively, fortifying the norms that underpin reciprocity, cooperation, and trust. It is assumed that an increase in social capital is characteristic of modern societies and supports female political participation and market efficiency. To the contrary, liberal theory assumes that social capital is from the beginning inherently female, thus making the world more harmonious. This modernist view is overlooking psycho-erotic hierarchies, power dynamics, and differences within communities and groups where an outstanding person is acknowledged as a leader. In his exposition of the reciprocity of super-ordination and subordination, Simmel has shown that this way of acting can be supportive as well as dangerous for social life. There is continuous oscillation between dissolution and reconstruction of the will to social power; a society without sex differences and gender conflicts would no longer be a dynamic but a utopian society of stagnating egalitarianism.

Recent research shows that Simmel's theory of gender relations is complex and future-oriented [23]. In the essay "The Relative and the Absolute in the Gender-Problem," published in *Philosophische Kultur* (1911), Simmel takes a new turn in his reflection on sex differences. In opposition to casual sex ("the relative"), sexuality connected with eroticism shapes the person as a whole and harmonizes all aspects of sexual behavior: "The absolute represents sexuality or eroticism as cosmological principle" [24]. The sex differences become manifest in the way sexuality is dealt with. According to Simmel, the sexual drive is dominant in men, whereas women perceive sexual arousal as secondary. This is because female sexuality rests more in itself and is consequently not in need of the relation to man. The being-in-itself of the "more profound female sexuality" refers to the potential maternity of the woman, but Simmel goes a step further in exalting female sexuality as a metaphysical principle which overcomes sexual relativity and elevates the absoluteness of the female Eros to the unity of being [25]. This corresponds to Simmel's late "ideal turn," which expounds how erotic love transcends the procreative telos of sexual intercourse and becomes an end in itself [26].

As one of the first sociologists to regard social interaction from the genetic point of view, which is marked by subjective experiences of basic instincts, Simmel is particularly convincing in his analysis of erotic love, the latter being "one of the great formative categories of existence." In his fragment *On Love*, Simmel starts out from the I-and-You-relationship as the prior one. With this starting point, Simmel's analysis is different and possibly more productive than all those conceptions of society that begin with isolated egos. The advantage of Simmel's view is to be seen in his most typical study of flirtation. He views flirtation as an alternation between consenting to and refusing bodily nearness. Flirtation is not only evident in the coquette who "neither resists, nor does she surrender" [27], but also in intellectual life. Communication is commonly connected with a sort of self-concealment in which a person hides his or her real purposes. Of course, flirtation was particularly significant in societies where rigid codes of conduct existed. It was a means by which the will to power could be exercised by women: "Flirtation is a means of enjoying this power in an enduring form." When men engage in flirtation, it becomes a game or a form of playing with reality. Like art, which places itself beyond reality, "flirtation also does no more than play with reality, yet it is still reality with which it plays." Flirtation is frequently a sign of dishonesty but it can also be "crystallized into a thoroughly positive way of acting."

In his multi-layered text *On Women, Sexuality & Love*, published posthumously in 1923, Simmel discusses flirtation as a generalized type of social interaction. According to Simmel, "to define flirtation as simply a 'passion for pleasing' is to confuse the means to an end with the desire for this end" [28]. The distinctiveness of the flirt lies in the means-end dialectic, similar to art for art's sake. The female part awakens desire by means of the presentation of her attractiveness but she does not consent in bodily nearness. In the flirt, the male part is induced to experience the inability to get what he wants. According to this, flirtation is the sophisticated form of the courtship process typically marked by a mixture of female surrender and coyness and of male aggression and frustration.

The foregoing reflections leave no doubt that for Simmel the fundamentally dualistic character of social interaction has its base in male-female polarity. Simmel acknowledges that women have basic erotic needs, but in their way of feeling they are "resting psychologically in themselves," which makes them less dependent on sexual activity. As a consequence, their ability to achieve goals is more centripetal, whereas men are centrifugal in their activities. This position of Simmel is confirmed by Max Scheler, who, at nearly the same time, states in the paper "Shame and the Feeling of Shame" that in women the tendency to objectivity is less developed than in men: "The female by nature has a less expansive, a more bound and ego-centered life. All thoughts, contents of perception and representation are not as strongly detached from bodily awareness and of the feeling of life as in men" [29]. Finally, Scheler calls women "the proper genius of life" and men the "genius of spirit."

In general terms, Simmel considers objective culture to be thoroughly male. But since the male character of Western culture "is grounded in a multifaceted interweaving of historical and psychological motives" and this "conflation of male values with values as such . . . is based on historical power relationships" [30], he falls back on the natural differentiation of men and women to explain why objective culture is more congruent with male personality. Why women do not get involved in objective culture is due to their personalities, which were then seen as less differentiated. Simmel points out that this situation will only change if women "accomplish something that men cannot do. This is the core of the entire problem, the pivotal point of the relationship between the women's movement and objective culture" [31]. Nevertheless, when Simmel goes on to examine the potential contributions of women to objective culture that would let them realize their own personalities within it, his examples are thoroughly traditional and conservative. Here, women's crucial contribution is to care for the home "in its state of serene, self-contained completeness" [32]. Simmel is almost forced into seeing the home as a positive cultural achievement by the psychological and metaphysical dichotomies with which he seeks to explain sociologically.

In the traditional view, maleness is associated with strength, contradiction, restlessness, becoming, and femaleness with beauty, harmony, stability, being. Simmel's polarized images of men and women are time-bound and thus outdated. On the other hand, Simmel has recognized the crucial problem of male and female personalities in social interaction, which later on dominated the vehement nature-nurture debate. This controversy seems to be overcome by modern theories of social learning, but in a fundamental sense it is still relevant as it proves the change from one radical position to the other in the ideologically programmed gender gap theories.

References

1. See Simmel, "Flirtation," *Georg Simmel: On Women, Sexuality and Love* (New Haven: Yale University Press, 1984).
2. See Wolff, *The Sociology of Georg Simmel*.
3. Christian Papilloud, *Sociology through Relation. Theoretical Assessments from the French Tradition* (New York: Palgrave Macmillan, 2018), 22.
4. See Wolff, *The Sociology of Georg Simmel*.
5. Simmel, "Flirtation."
6. See Simmel "Female Culture," *Georg Simmel: On Women, Sexuality and Love* (New Haven: Yale University Press, 1984).
7. Max Marcuse, ed., *Handwörterbuch der Sexualwissenschaft* (Berlin: Walter de Gruyter, 2001). See, e.g., the article "Erotik" or "Geschlechtsmerkmale."
8. Rüdiger Lautmann, *Soziologie der Sexualität* (Weinheim: Juventa, 2002).
9. Simmel, *Sociology: Inquiries into the Construction of Social Forms*, trans. Anthony J Blasi, Anton K. Jacobs, and Mathew Kanjirathinkal (Leiden and Boston: Brill, 2009).
10. See Wolff, *The Sociology of Georg Simmel*: "On the one hand, sexual intercourse is the most intimate and personal process, but on the other hand, it is absolutely general, absorbing the very personality in the service of the species and in the universal organic claim of nature. The psychological secret of this act lies in its double character of being both wholly personal and wholly impersonal" (131).
11. Wolff, *The Sociology of Georg Simmel*, 325.
12. Bronislaw Malinowski, *A Scientific Theory of Culture and Other Essays* (New York: Oxford University Press, 1960), VIII.
13. Edward O. Wilson, *Sociobiology: The New Synthesis* (Cambridge, MA and London: The Belknap Press of Harvard University Press, 1975).
14. Ferdinand Fellmann and Rebecca Walsh, "From Sexuality to Eroticism: The Making of the Human Mind," *Advances in Anthropology*, 6, 11–24.
15. Georg Simmel, "Die Wendung zur Idee," *Lebensanschauung: Vier metaphysische Kapitel* (Berlin: Duncker and Humblot), 62.
16. Levine, *On Individuality and Social Forms*, 298.
17. Wolff, *The Sociology of Georg Simmel*, 404f.
18. Simmel, *Das individuelle Gesetz*, 116.
19. Simmel, "The Conflict in Modern Culture," 389.
20. See Wolff, *The Sociology of Georg Simmel*.
21. Ulrich Beck, *Risikogesellschaft. Auf dem Weg in eine andere Moderne* (Frankfurt: Suhrkamp, 1996).
22. Robert D. Putnam, *Bowling Alone* (New York: Simon and Schuster, 2000).
23. For an overview, see Guenther Roth "Biographische Aspekte der amerikanischen Simmelrezeption," in *Georg Simmels große Soziologie*, Hartmann Tyrell et al. (ed.), 367–393.
24. Simmel, "Das Relative und das Absolute im Geschlechter-problem," *Philosophische Kultur* (Leipzig: Verlag von Dr. Werner Klinkhardt, 1911), 72. This sounds like an echo of the German philosopher of art, Friedrich Theodor Vischer, whose work was well known to Simmel. In his novel *Auch einer* Vischer developed his concept of femininity as follows: "The female in her light-dark being is a mysterious unity of the world-poles nature and spirit."
25. Ibid., 75. This is in agreement with the view of the Russian-born German writer Lou Andreas-Salomé, who frequented Simmel's salon in Berlin. After having studied in Vienna with Sigmund Freud, with whom she exchanged letters, she was one of the first women to write psychoanalytically on female sexuality.
26. Simmel, "Die Wendung zur Idee," 60.
27. Simmel, "Flirtation."
28. Ibid., 104.

29. Max Scheler "Über Scham und Schamgefühl," *Schriften aus dem Nachlass Band 10* (Bern: Franke, 1957), 146.
30. David Frisby and Mike Featherstone, ed., *Simmel on Culture: Selected Writings* (London: Sage, 1997), 51.
31. Ibid., 53.
32. Ibid., 49.

Chapter 5
Personality and Individual Differences

5.1 The Concept of Personality

The foregoing chapters have made clear that personality is a key concept of Simmel's thought. Personality represents a mental state that is in no way always experienced without complications. Since the beginning, philosophers and psychologists have thus been disturbed by the consciousness of self that involves a stream of thought, each part of which is experienced as "I" [1]. In certain situations, people ask the existential question: "Who am I?" The person asking this question is not asking a trivial question that can be answered with information about biographical data or one's bodily or personality traits. The "who" being asked about refers to self-realization without ever really knowing the meaning of selfhood. Only one thing is unquestionable: human personality is permeated by conflicts. The social type best representing the structure of personality, which is constantly changing yet always the same, is found in Simmel's essay "The Adventurer." Here, Simmel states that the adventurer represents a form of life that, more than all others, is erotic. Referring to Casanova, Simmel characterizes the form of the adventure as the interplay of two elements: "conquering force and unextortable concession, winning by one's own abilities and dependence on the luck which something incalculable outside ourselves bestows on us" [2]. Simmel states that the two poles of conquest and grace are arranged differently in men and women, and he concludes that the analogies to erotic love make adventure a form of life for young people. To what extent the erotic dimension of Simmel's concept of personality is valid may be shown in the different contexts where Simmel is using this concept.

Already in chapter seven of the second volume of *Introduction to Moral Science*, titled "Unity and the Conflict of Ends," Simmel turns to the unity of personality in connection with the concept of the supreme good that unites all psychological purposes. Although human action is determined by conflicts, the assumption of a higher end is not excluded. Consequently, Simmel holds tight to the concept of personality whose unity is more than the sum of single purposes. This unity is

F. Fellmann, *Rethinking Georg Simmel's Social Philosophy*, SpringerBriefs in Sociology, https://doi.org/10.1007/978-3-030-57351-5_5

experienced in the feeling of life that organizes the emotions into sentiments. Simmel states that in the eudaemonistic style of life the organization of emotional attitudes is a process of crystallization of subjective impulses into objective forms of moral obligation. More so in the erotic hedonist, who experiences love affairs as an increase in self-evaluation.

In *The Philosophy of Money* Simmel distinguishes between the principle of objectivity and the principle of personality [3]. Personality refers to a certain person who is distinguished from others through his or her properties and accordingly acknowledged. This acknowledgment does not result from a single property but from the reciprocity of different character traits that reinforce each other: "It is not that it is this *or* that trait that makes a unique personality of man, but that he is this *and* that trait" [4]. In the formation of the personality, the acquisition of property plays a central role. Following William James, who defines the Self "the sum total of all he can call his, not only his body and his psychic powers, but his clothes and his house, his wife and children … his yacht and bank-account. All these things give him the same emotions" [5]. Simmel is concerned with working out the interplay of the subjective and the objective factor and he stresses that money increases this twofold function of property in the formation of the personality. Property is an external object that releases emotions and impulses in the owner; it is crystallized in the form of money. "This concept of property as a mere enlargement of the personality is not refuted but rather is strongly confirmed by cases in which the self-awareness of the personality [*Persönlichkeitsgefühl*: feeling of personality, FF] has been transposed from the core of the Ego to its surrounding layers, to property" [6]. *The Philosophy of Money* shows the wide extent of the meaning of property:

> That self-awareness [*Ichgefühl*: Ego-feeling, FF] has transcended its immediate boundaries, and has become rooted in objects that only indirectly concern it, really proves to what extent property as such means nothing other than the extension of the personality into objects and, through its domination of them, the gaining of its sphere of influence. This explains the strange phenomenon that sometimes the sum total of possessions [*des Habens*: of having, FF] appears to be identical with the totality of the personality [des Seins: of being, FF] [7].

The psychoanalyst Erich Fromm was familiar with Simmel's works and agreed with Simmel's view of sociological psychology. In his famous book *To Have or to Be?* (1976) Fromm complains that modern society has become materialistic and prefers "having" to "being." He states that the great promise of unlimited material abundance and personal freedom failed due to the selfishness and greed of people to increase their property. In the industrial age, the development of the economic system is no longer determined by the question of what is good for the personality, but rather of what is good for the growth of the system. In view of Simmel's position, the strict opposition of "to be" and "to have" seems to be exaggerated. Here, Simmel's view is more realistic.

For Simmel, the feeling of individual self-sufficiency or inner independence results from living in large groups, where the individual feels isolated yet independent: "Stated in purely logical terms, independence is something other than non-dependence … Individual freedom is not a pure inner condition of an isolated subject, but rather a phenomenon of correlation which loses its meaning when its opposite is absent" [8].

In the chapter "Individual Freedom" Simmel explains how the economy is changing the image of man. According to the principle of reciprocity of different characters, the "economic man" of the modern age has gained personal freedom in his work life. The modern worker no longer feels dependent on the company because of the money equivalent of his performance. Simmel considers this independence a general phenomenon that applies not only to the working world but also the world of aesthetic production.

The dialectic of objectivity and subjectivity is the result of a never-ending process of cultural evolution. This process is analogous to the emotional development of the child into an adult. The small group of two adult persons connected by intimate relations leads to erotic life as the undercurrent of sociation. In the chapter "The Money Equivalent of Personal Values" Simmel shows that money is a means for holding together different characters, but money is never a good mediator in true love between man and woman because the value of personality is absolute [9].

Concerning personal values, Simmel distinguishes between women and men, a difference which he traces back to sexuality. The impersonal act of sexual intercourse is experienced by women "as the most personal, including her intimacy." Generally speaking, for the woman "the generic and the personal coincide" [10]. The materials Simmel cites show that he explains the difference between male and female personality in a similar way to modern sociobiology. Feminists initially rejected the new science but later on Margret Mead confessed that she would lay more emphasis on the human's specific biological inheritance from the evolution of earlier forms of individuation.

The difficulty to produce a convincing view of personality is a topic in *The Problems of the Philosophy of History* (1907). Simmel modifies the Kantian theory of knowledge, replacing Kant's "unity of consciousness" with the "unity of personality" as the a priori of historical knowledge. Simmel understands personality as the set of characteristics that an individual possesses, which differs from those of a person (legal) or subject (epistemological). In this sense, the unity of personality gives the problem of personal identity a new angle. Simmel takes into consideration that both the historian and the historical actor are beings in the world. Consequently, to explain the special subject-object relation, Simmel refers to the dialectic of nearness and distance in human interaction. In this process of understanding, subjectivity and objectivity are interrelated, so that the unity of personality becomes a heuristic function in intersubjective mind-reading. The unity is not a logical one, not a form of thought that is brought to the experience from outside, but the unfolding of the subjective feeling itself [11]. This functions in the feedback model, which is always at work in intersubjective communication. Simmel speaks of the "dynamic role" of intersubjectivity in the formation of acquired character in life history. Simmel calls the unique, intermediate state between subjectivism and objectivism "suprapersonality of the psychological relations," a formulation that corresponds to the concept of truth developed in the first chapter of *The Philosophy of Money*.

In his monography *Goethe* (1913) Simmel highlights "the general of his personality" [12]. Personality, interpreted as the "unity of life," stands for the creativity of the poet. His poetry encompasses the "development of his whole, substantial personal life" [13]. Simmel deals here extensively with the erotic elements in Goethe's personality, and states that the erotic feeling is the inner core of his life history [14]. In his analysis of the interplay of egoism and devotion, Simmel uses reciprocity as a psychological concept.

In *Rembrandt* Simmel uses the word "personality" only scarcely. Instead, he often speaks of the "unity of life," which is more than the sum of the parts and means absolute continuity [15]. This unity of life is expressed in the human face, whose meaning is depicted visually in Rembrandt's portraits. The creative power "emerges as immediate unity out of the deepest creative ground of his personality" [16]. Simmel locates the deep ground in the stream of life, which is composed of waves. The waves, one can say with the Austrian poet Grillparzer, are the waves of sea and love.

In the essay "The Problem of the Religious Situation" Simmel discusses the psychology of religious faith. Mental need and fulfillment regulate subjective experience and lead us back to the religious background of his concept of personality. The human as a being with needs is full of contradictions; only in God can we find the complete unity and coherence of all aspects. Soul's longing for this unity is the expression of the two origins of religious life, namely, the sensual and mental. Simmel points out how this original structure is analogous to Plato's definition of Eros as the sun of poverty and richness [17].

This overview of the different aspects and applications of Simmel's concept of personality demonstrates that he has given a new meaning to the idealistic philosophy of consciousness, which is most strongly expressed in erotic life: self-experience ends the rigid opposition of life and form and returns personal identity to the dialectic relation between sensuality and intellect. This becomes true in Simmel's picture of Platonic Diotima, "who refers to Eros beyond the desire of enjoyment to the essential drive: to create and to preserve our being in artefacts, bodily and mental, outside of ourselves" [18]. In other words, Diotima, who is bound to her beauty, her own personality, uses all her powers to fabricate a mythical creature. She thus represents the metaphysical background of Simmel's idea of personality, which is crucial for his image of man. But there remains a serious problem. Eros has multiple identities in his creative personality, which would fall apart without a firm hold in a true love relationship.

5.2 Horizons of Personal Identity

A man, therefore, who gets so far as making the supposed unity of the self two-fold is already almost a genius, in any case a most exceptional and interesting person. In reality, however, every ego, so far from being a unity is in the highest degree a manifold world, a constellated heaven, a chaos of forms, of states and stages, of inheritances and potentialities.

It appears to be a necessity as imperative as eating and breathing for everyone to be forced to regard this chaos as a unity and to speak of his ego as though it were a one-fold and clearly detached and fixed phenomenon. Even the best of us shares the delusion.

This passage was taken from Herman Hesse's *Steppenwolf* (1927), a novel which has captivated young readers for generations. It throws a poetic light on a serious philosophical problem: for flexible, modern day humans, personal identity is not an obvious given, but it is a task that the individual can only solve with extreme difficulty if there is no interpersonal communication. Philosophers of subjectivity have only recently moved the role of the other in the construction of the self into the foreground. For the philosopher of religion Emmanuel Levinas, it is the face of the other in distress that makes demands on me to accept responsibility for him, without which there would be no justice. And the "hermeneutics of the self" by the French phenomenologist Paul Ricoeur conceives of others as the audience of a promise, through which the person making the promise becomes conscious of his own selfhood. Behind these and other similar conceptions, which are all influenced by humanism, there are in any case hidden preconditions that are in need of clarification.

The problems associated with personal identity being discussed here were, notably, already recognized by the ancient Greeks. This is why the Delphic Oracle challenged humans to attain self-knowledge. This self-knowledge allows humans to hold up the objective information about themselves against their subjective expectations (i.e., what they want to be and what they ought to be). The question of personal identity thus links that which is factual and normative in a way that sets humans apart from all other animals as creatures whose existence depends on their mental state, both conscious and unconscious.

There are times when we wish we were another person. This is, of course, an innocent wish whose fulfillment would amount to, strictly speaking, one ending his own existence and another taking his place. In reality, however, we only want the other's traits or to live in different circumstances. To say that we are dissatisfied with ourselves, and, despite the logical impossibility, that we want to be someone else appears to be more than a linguistic inaccuracy. Hiding behind this is the philosophical problem of the unity of self-consciousness. The classical philosophy of the subject differentiates between an unchanging, substantial "I" and its changing representations, or accidents. But this model obviously does not do justice to self-experience.

William James, one of the leading thinkers of the late nineteenth century in the United States, proposed in his *Essays in Radical Empircism* (1912) an alternative answer to the classical question about the unity of consciousness. He stated: "It surely can be nothing intrinsic in the individual experience. It is their way of behaving towards each other, their system of relations" [19]. This relativism is due to the nature of humans, which is, unlike animals, not fixed, and it is often experienced by individuals as a kind of disturbance. In order to fix personal identity, there must be a balance between being, wanting, and duty, which all compete for the human's self-understanding. The three categories create an area of conflict in which it is not always possible to achieve balance. Herein lies the old, famous conflict between duty and inclination but also between inclinations that are mutually exclusive. This experience of difference, which can never be entirely done away with, makes answers to questions about the self considerably more difficult to find than those dealing with moral questions about what one ought to do, which seems simple in comparison. This experience brings about, above all, the "problematic natures" that cause the reflective self to exist in a state of permanent uncertainty about who he or she really is. One must always be prepared to be surprised by oneself, and effort is required to avoid becoming the pathological case of a split personality.

The problem of identity is always latent in the individual. Conditions may arise causing the question to become urgent. The situational dependency of personal identity first comes to mind. In normal, everyday life things typically run as usual—external and internal stability are mutually dependent. Each person plays a role according to the expectations that society puts on them. But there are, of course, exceptional situations brought about by unforeseen occurrences, especially due to career failures or family separations. Folk psychology refers to these situations using the known and feared expression "things always seem to happen when you least expect them to." In any case, these situations occur more often than one would prefer. It is the moment when you feel as if the carpet is moving from underneath you and you try to find solid ground to stand on. Personal identity is connected to the relative stability of intimate relationships with family and friends; and when this stability is lost, individuals must strive to find a new way of living.

For the preservation of individuality, humans depend on boundaries with respect to others. For Simmel, individuality preserves relative distances between individuals. If someone surrenders him or herself entirely over to another—whether this is a person or an idea—they lose their own individuality as well as their identity. But the necessity of boundaries in no way cancels out an intimate relationship with another. Humans need intimate relations to confirm their personal identity. Personal identity constituted by the relation to a beloved is paradoxical. Each lover wants to internalize the other, or to "devour" the other, but no one wants to be devoured by the other. A permanent struggle therefore emerges, which Simmel referred to as the dialectical relation of nearness and distance.

In the discussion of the meaning of communication between individuals, "narcissism" comes into play. In his important essay entitled "On Narcissism" (1914) Freud states that narcissism is not merely a form of sexual perversion but a basic element of normal love. The beginning of sexual love is self-love where libido is concentrated in the ego: primary narcissism. When libido is turned outwards it becomes object-love. The consequence is a permanent conflict between self-love and object-love in the development of the individual. This conflict is at the source of the individual self and stands for the transformation of primary narcissism into spontaneous affirmation of the beloved other without sacrificing one's own integrity. This remarkable reciprocity between the love of self and the love of others is the new concept of narcissism, which tends to be identified with the whole development of the individual self.

What Freud called "narcissism of small differences" (*Narzissmus der kleinen Differenzen*) was analyzed by Simmel in his essay *Zur Psychologie der Scham* (1901). He states that each individual is separated from others by a taboo of personal secrecy. He refers to the old Jewish law that allows bigamy but forbids relatives living together in a house.

Another horizon of personal identity that extends beyond personal life concerns the economic and political structures. Whereas James as psychologist and philosopher referred to consciousness, asking whether it exists, Simmel as sociologist and philosopher is concerned with the development of individuality in society. Here, the distinction between open and closed societies is crucial. In closed and traditional societies, the individual remains bound to collective behavior and thinking patterns. This means that individuality is completely absorbed by role identity—a state in which humans are the mere "functionaries" of anonymous institutional structures.

The situation is different in open societies, where emancipated individuals can determine how to organize their lives. "The End of Role Models" (Alexander Mitscherlich) is first apparent in the dissolution of the traditional family structure. Mother and father no longer act as obvious, recognized authorities for the child. This has led to the "fatherless society," which can now be appended with "motherless society," since mothers increasingly become their child's confidant, especially daughters, with whom they talk about relationship problems. The transformation is subtle and is specific to particular social strata, but it cannot be overlooked: there is a developmental tendency in the direction of an egalitarian individualism, which creates new horizons of individuality and personality for children in the same way as for adults.

5.3 Identity and Individuality

This rough sketch of the parameters of identity has shown that a workable concept of personal identity cannot be formed without a clarification of individuality. Simmel's principle of individuality is a good guide. From an objective standpoint, the relation between identity and individuality is relatively easy to explain. Things such as persons can undoubtedly be identified by establishing their characteristics. This is used in the term "numerical identity," which Quine disguised in his famous statement "no entity without identity" [20]. To make an absolute spatio-temporal identification would require an all-knowing observer who can oversee all places at all times. Externally viewed, identity requires individuality in the sense of discriminability. Leibniz gets to the point exactly in his famous principle of the "identity of indiscernibles" [21].

If one shifts from the objective standpoint to subjective experience, identity and individuality do not coincide. Aside from pathological cases, no one confuses himself for another. That we can say "I" does not, however, require us to have knowledge of our characteristics or our life history. "Characteristics" are understood here not only as external traits but also as internal ones, thus, as that which is referred to as a "character's characteristics." Here, the subjective standpoint is in no way superior to the view of the observer. But the ignorance of one's own inner world does not change the fact that I experience myself as identical to me. We are dealing with self-sameness, which one always has as the experiencing subject. It forms the unavoidable reference point of personal identity.

Phenomenologically speaking, self-experience shows us an interesting fact: Even if we only know little about ourselves and in extreme cases nothing at all, we still feel ourselves as a person in a certain state. To this belongs spatial localization, or where we find ourselves, as well as temporal localization, the "now" in which we are living. Contrary to Husserl who stressed the inner consciousness of time, in *Sociology* Simmel explicitly addresses the social production of space, the spatial dimensions of social interaction [22]. Simmel's seminal sociology of space had a great influence on the Marxist sociologist Henri Lefebvre, who accomplished the spatial turn in the social sciences [23]. *The Urban Revolution* in the late 1960s was concerned with the transformation of "the city" into "the urban," which culminated in the "complete urbanization of society" and thus developed Simmel's analysis of urban life at the end of *The Philosophy of Money*. Both theorists can be identified with a hermeneutic approach. One can speak with Simmel of a kind of "life feeling" that is bound to the body like the feeling of space and time. Identity therefore does not remain with numerical agency; in self-experience persons become aware of their individuality as something that is unique to self-feeling.

The ideal of authentic individuality pursued by Simmel sociologically has been developed by Freud psychoanalytically [24]. Psychoanalysis sees internal sense as primary to external sense. Internal consciousness contains no data, but it does contain qualities, such as joy or sorrow. Freud is moving on a different track, but he ultimately comes near to Simmel's principle of individuality. Freud reconstructs subjectivity as a "psychical apparatus" in which different authorities fight each other for supremacy: id, ego, and superego. Freud transfers these authorities of individuality to the relation between the pleasure principle and the reality principle. Thus the "ego" as the controlling authority corresponds to what usually is called the "intellect" or "knowledge."

If one approaches Freud's description of the psyche using Simmel's sociological approach, Freud's conception of the psyche as the balance between unconscious wishes and conscious norms is in any case near to genetic phenomenology. On the one hand, for Freud the individual is merely a short proliferation of the germline, so that the ego's only function is to continue the germline. The developmental history of the ego therefore reflects the libido, which has a phylogenetic nature. On the other hand, Freud said that ego individuality goes deep into the "dark id," the core of human nature, where the longing for an object of love emerges. "The finding of an object is in fact the refinding of it"; this key sentence in Freud's theory of sexuality shows that he considered erotic love to be a late embodiment of infantile sexuality. Freud considers the relation between infantile and adult love to be the source of the unity of the individual; and the survival of the individual depends on the success of this balance. If the balance fails, it results in a dangerous division of the ego, which has been described by Ronald D. Laing in *The Divided Self* (1964).

The division of the self is not only a pathological case but can be found in social interaction as well. It is interesting to notice that cultural identity is closely linked to the personal appearance of people. In the view of European liberalism and individualism, a veiled Muslim woman appears not as an individual so much as a representative of the species. The lack of personal self-expression can be seen especially in the slow way of walking of an Islamic woman, who would never act the part of the American Pretty Woman. Henry Miller in 1939 writes about his girlfriend Mona in New York City: "What a walk! It's not a walk, it's a glider. Tall, stately, full bodied, self-possessed, she cuts the smoke and jazz and red-light glow like the queen mother and all the slippery Babylonian whores" [25]. Though this example seems to be far-fetched and is typical of Miller's eroticism, it is actually central for the understanding of personal and national identity. In *The Adventurer* Simmel states that "a love affair is an 'adventure' only for man" [26]. But in our time women have learned the erotic drive of the adventurer as well. One can say in general that in order to understand how a society feels about itself one has to consider the role of women in public and private life, which do not necessarily coincide.

References

1. William James, *The Principles of Psychology, Vol. 1* (New York: Dover Publications, 1950), 291–401.
2. Simmel, "The Adventurer," in Donald N. Levine, *On Individuality and Social Forms* (Chicago: University of Chicago, 1971), 195.
3. Simmel, *The Philosophy of Money*, 307.
4. Ibid., 319.
5. James, *The Principles of Psychology*, 291.
6. Simmel, *The Philosophy of Money*, 349.
7. Ibid.
8. Ibid., 322.
9. Ibid., 384ff.
10. Ibid., 409.
11. Simmel, *The Problems of the Philosophy of History*, 11f.
12. Simmel, "Goethe," 257.
13. Ibid., 229.
14. Ibid., 198ff.
15. Simmel, *Philosophy of Art: Rembrandt, Ein kunstphilosophischer Versuch* (Leipzig: Wolff, 1919), 1ff.
16. Ibid., 200.
17. Simmel, "Das Problem der religiosen Lage," *Philosophische Kultur. Gesammelte Essays* (Leipzig: Klinkhardt, 1911), 233.
18. Simmel, "Goethe," 102.
19. William James, *Essays in Radical Empiricism* (Lincoln and London: University of Nebraska Press, 1996), 154.
20. Willard Van Orman Quine, *Word and Object* (Cambridge, MA: The MIT Press, 2013).
21. Gottfried Leibniz, "Discourse on Metaphysics," in Leroy Loemker, *Philosophical Papers and Letters* (Dordecht: D. Reidel, 1969).
22. See "The Stranger" in Wolff, *The Sociology of Georg Simmel.*

23. Henri Lefebvre, *La révolution urbaine* (Paris: Gallimard, 1970).
24. Sigmund Freud, *Introductory Lectures on Psychanalysis*, transl. J. Strachey (New York: W.W. Norton & Co, 1995).
25. Henry Miller, *Tropic of Capricorn* (New York: Grove Press, 1961), 342.
26. Simmel, *On Individuality and Social Forms,* 195.

Chapter 6
Individual Ethics

6.1 Is and Ought

Throughout his life Simmel was concerned with the ethical implications of culture. In the first chapter of *Introduction to Moral Science* (1893), "The Ought," Simmel argues against the Kantian categorical imperative because it does not heed the concrete situations of human actions. In its stead, Simmel proposes a eudaemonistic justification of moral norms through natural needs and sensual drives, which are explained in detail in chapter four titled "Happiness." In his later period, under the influence of Bergson's philosophy of life, Simmel gives preference to obligations that develop according to the totality of one's individual life, comprising happiness and pain. Along these lines Simmel develops his idea of individual morality, which reconciles the general and the individual. The shift from the early Introduction to *The Law of the Individual* (1913) is analogue to the step from the first to the second edition of his *The Problems of the Philosophy of History* (see Chap. 1). In both cases Simmel has taken an idealistic turn, which surpasses the mere behavioristic point of view.

The usual epistemic justification of moral norms is complemented by emotional intelligence, which reacts to biological facts and to characteristics of the human psyche. Simmel takes into account specific moral response patterns, thus pointing out the existence of sex differences. Women appear to be emotionally motivated to behave in an ethically adequate manner, whereas men's values appear to be of a cognitive nature. Sex differences as the basis of morality are nowadays outdated but Simmel in his observation of everyday life was well aware that men and women feel and act in different ways.

In modern ethics—which is heavily influenced by analytical thinking—Simmel's principle of individuality and the formula of the individual law are not explicitly present. Discourse ethics considers normative truths to be the core of egalitarian communication. But the argument against egalitarianism is that if everyone had the same participation cost, there would be no comparative advances and no one would gain from communicating with each other. Competitive interaction enriches individuals because they are unequal in character traits and talents—whether these differences are innate or culturally developed. In view of the undeniable individual differences one cannot fail to notice that the current discussion of moral situations and dilemmas points to conclusions similar to those reached by Simmel in his relativism of cultural norms.

In his Logos-article "Das individuelle Gesetz" (1913/extended 1918) (literally translated "Individual Law") Simmel argues against Kant's theory that there is a single moral obligation derived from the concept of duty (categorical imperative). Already in his *Introduction to the Science of Ethics* (1892/1893) Simmel points out that Kantian "duty," like physical laws, applies only to rational agents. But humans are not only guided by reason but by emotions as well. Among the basic emotions like anger, fear, disgust, etc., love is unique, as it must be shared by a loving partner. Only in a state of loving and being loved can individuals experience themselves as whole persons with rights and obligations to others. This is the primordial root of ethics, which does not regard exclusively what a person does but what he or she is. One's being or character may be better than one's actions, and concrete ethics have to take that into account.

The extended version of the Logos-article appeared in Simmel's final work, *The View of Life* (1918). Here, Simmel replaces the opposition of life and ought with reality and ought, both being two modes of personal life with equal rights. By inverting Kant's categorical imperative, Simmel is convinced he has produced an ethics of authentic individuality. While Kant's moral imperative is universal to all individuals but particular to their discrete acts, Simmel's individual law is particular to each individual but universal to all the individual's acts. Linguistically Simmel likes to speak of "lawfulness" (*Gesetzlichkeit*) in the legal sense instead of "law" in the sense of laws of nature. Consequently, Simmel's statements in the *Law of the Individual* can be considered an articulation of an ethical level that is in agreement with his genetical approach to social philosophy.

Law of the Individual conceptualizes a decisive moment of legal organization woven into social relationships. Simmel opens the way to fold social relations back into the analysis of one's relationship with oneself and explains how forms of association are shaped by forms of self-relation. Thus, the theoretical gulf between Simmel's philosophy of life and his sociology, which commentators usually hold apart, is bridged. The result is a distinctively Simmelean approach to an ethics of individuality in the frame of social philosophy as a view of life. To be sure, normative conclusions cannot be deduced from descriptive premises. This would be a social fallacy analogous to the well-known naturalistic fallacy. Simmel does not deduce "ought" from "is" of social facts but from the way they are experienced by the actors. This experience is a representative one that forms personality as a process of self-regulation through self-images to fulfill emotional desires and devices. At first sight, this resembles the so-called "natural normativity" introduced by modern primatologists to explain that animals feel an impulse to help other animals [1]. But this impulse to act in a functionally adequate manner of cooperation is not comparable to the human moral obligations that emerge in relation to personal life history.

Here, erotic love is a prominent instance of the dialectic of nearness and distance. Simmel speaks of a "double life," the real and ideal, as the root of moral obligation [2]. In other words, "ought" is the highest level in the ongoing process of individualization and social integration.

6.2   Freedom in a Situation

It has been objected that the law of the individual is a logical contradiction in itself and opens the door to subjective arbitrariness. This criticism overlooks that for Simmel the individual is always in a situation. This reminds one of Jean-Paul Sartre's concept of *situation* in *Being and Nothingness* (1943), where he famously said that there is *freedom* only in a *situation*, and there is a *situation* only through freedom. The situation is never neutral but implies a principle of differentiating between right and wrong. This principle may be called "appropriate behavior" corresponding to the character of the participants. According to the *kathecon* of Stoic philosophy, each being must carry out the action according to nature. Nature here means the whole world, which is regarded as a harmonious cosmos guided by reason. For Simmel, thinking in a more biological way apart from teleology, nature comes near to the complexities of human erotic life. Consequently, social action is convenient if it is based on a realistic appraisal of basic human instincts, which transcend the mere pleasure principle. The criterion of right and wrong is not as in Kant the logical consistency of the maxim but it is the self-image formed by the individual through living and loving. This corresponds to Simmel's statement that humans are the only beings which have to justify their existence. This task of moral justification results from the fact that we are what we pretend to be, so we must be careful about what our image looks like.

Simmel thus distances himself from the hedonist ethical theory he still held in the *Introduction to Moral Science*. He now tries to give back to the individual the freedom of decision independent of the pressures of the outer environment. Here, Simmel follows Henri Bergson's concept of freedom. In his *Essay sur les donnés immediates de la conscience* (1889) (Engl. *Time and Free Will*), the French philosopher describes the emergence of self-consciousness. Ever since Descartes, philosophers have typically connected consciousness with reason and intelligence, neglecting its embeddedness in bodily experience and emotionality. In opposition, Bergson suggests that the immediate data of consciousness, the absolute starting point, as it were, is "duration." Bergson argued that philosophers traditionally confused time with its spatial representation. In reality, duration is un-extended yet heterogeneous, and so its moments cannot be arranged as a succession of distinct parts, with one part causing the next. Based on this, Bergson concluded that freedom is not a breaking up of the chain of cause and effect but the concentration of all past moments in an extraordinary experience of presentational immediacy. In this primordial state of mind, appearance and reality are one and the same. In states of emotional intensity, objective time is cancelled out, and facing one's past and building one's future coincide.

In his article "Henri Bergson" (1914) Simmel resumes Bergson's philosophy of life [3]. Bergson's metaphysical concept of life is indebted to biological vitalism. Life contains a surplus of energy as the last ground of the world. Simmel writes, "It is life itself . . . with its urge and will to surpass, with its changing and differentiating, that affords the dynamic for the whole movement, but which being formless can become real through formation only" [4]. Life becomes the border concept of the original unity of being before all differentiations.

To be sure, the metaphysical concept of life is of no use for phenomenological research and has brought forth dubious results regarding the world of social life. But it has opened up new ways for the modern feeling of life. Bergson's original insight consists in the fact that life is not in time but time is produced by the process of life. In this way, life is considered an organizing principle that will stop the increasing mechanization of industrial societies. Simmel, too, is fascinated by this idea. But as much as he follows Bergson, he maintains a critical distance from his *élan vital*. Simmel criticizes Bergson for not sufficiently taking into account the inner inconsistency of life [5]. The inconsistency lies in the fact that life is always generating forms that inhibit the further development of sociality. This conflict reminds one of Schopenhauer's "view of the inner contradiction of the will to life to itself," which Simmel considers irretrievable [6]. Simmel states that "every human is an Adam because everybody is once expulsed from the paradise of warm feelings" [7]. The return to the totality of life is blocked for modern man as it was blocked for Adam and Eve after the Fall. Nevertheless, in life as a stream of impressions and emotions the person experiences a need for inner freedom that overcomes mechanical determinism. In exceptional moments of existence, the totality of life history is experienced as "duration" that generates a feeling of self-validation by showing an exemplary attitude toward others. Here, the genetic scheme of the emergence of social values reaches its highest level. Consequently, the task of ethics is not to prescribe moral actions that ought to be done, but to investigate the oftentimes dissonant emotional and practical demands of social behavior. It follows from this that the actions of human individuals are subject to a law that is both universal and private.

6.3   Individual Law of Eros

As the German philosopher Hans Blumenberg has already shown, Simmel's idea of an individual law elaborated in *Law of the Individual* was already evident in *The Philosophy of Money* [8]. Simmel viewed money as a symbolic form that enables an understanding of life-history perspectives on personality. This view derives from his discovery of the close relation between the economy and human passions. Their common feature is the dynamic of the will to live. This structural equivalence turns money into a basic metaphor of human existence, which connects subjective and objective culture. Here, the objectivity of norms is bound to subjective experiences and evaluations.

In this sense Simmel can describe the effectiveness of the individual law as an expression of the will to believe in a better world. This applies not only to social and political situations but to privacy as well. The human body is constantly sending out signals to its social companions. Among the overall signals, the invitations to sexual intimacy are the most intense. In erotic love the carnal element is present but sexual arousal transcends itself akin to a religious feeling. The individual law hence redeems the inner representation of a person's yearning. This holds particularly true for the way women and men experience and judge an intimate relation.

In the late text "Eros, Platonic and Modern" Simmel holds tight to the primacy of individuality and points out the structural analogy between the individual law and erotic love: ". . . so there must be something like an individual law of eroticism in the incomparable relation between incomparable individuals" [9]. This is notoriously the case in erotic sentiment characteristic for women. The well-known German philosophical anthropologist Michael Landmann remarks that Simmel has attributed the realization of the individual law to women [10]. Thus, female erotic life turns out to be at the root of concrete morality. According to Margarete Susman, the fact that Simmel attributes the individual law to women shows "that the woman and Eros in all relations and forms have always occupied Simmel's thinking" [11]. Here, sex differences show different ways of seeing. However universal reason may be, human emotional intelligence is still more basic. In this respect Simmel's concept of individual law confirms sex as a cultural force.

It may be recapitulated that the libidinous undercurrent of Simmel's conception of social life has seldom been noticed. Neither sociologists nor later interpreters have payed sufficient attention to the fact that Simmel's appearance was an erotic one shaped by public appearance. As mentioned in the Introduction, Simmel had a life-long secret mistress with whom he was leading a double life parallel to his bourgeois existence. Of course, Simmel's theories are not a direct projection of his personal life, but his erotic eccentricity and social nonconformity shed light on his way of seeing the world. On the one hand, Simmel's love affair conformed to the libidinal structure of his personality, and, on the other, his secret was not socially correct and is to be regarded as a moral failure.

Simmel's fixation on the subjective point of view is reflected in the later evaluations of his legacy. Theodor Litt, for example, has appreciated the individualism but pointed out that he misses the relation to the community [12]. In the essay *Die geistige Gestalt Georg Simmels* (1959), Margarete Susman also stresses that in the individual law the relation between the individual and society is mainly represented from the first-person perspective. Thus in Susman's view, it does not correspond to modern theories of communication emphasizing social perspectives.

These criticisms are partly justified. But Simmel's reliance on the stream of life does include the experience of others. In this Heraclitean view nothing is solid, everything moves, even love, which is held as eternal. "Hold on to love, do what love requires" is how the Simmelean "individual imperative" of ethics as an art of living would sound. Defining flirtation as a generalized type of social interaction,

Simmel goes beyond any one-sided approach and considers the interrelation between nearness and distance in sexual behavior in all its complexity, marking and explaining convergent and divergent aspects. This approach can be helpful in attenuating movements that might disturb ethically balanced relationships between men and women.

References

1. Franz de Waal, "Natural normativity: The 'is' and 'ought' of animal behavior," *Behaviour* 151 (2014), 181–204.
2. Simmel, *Lebensanschauung*, 186.
3. Simmel, "Henri Bergson," *Zur Philosophie der Kunst* (Potsdam: Kiepenheuer, 1922), 127–145.
4. Simmel, *Das Individuelle Gesetz*, 150.
5. Simmel, "Henri Bergson," 138, 144.
6. Arthur Schopenhauer, *Die Welt als Wille und Vorstellung, Sämtliche Werke Band I* (Frankfurt: Suhrkamp, 1986), 454.
7. Simmel, *Goethe* (Leipzig: Verlag von Klinkhardt and Biermann, 1913), 208.
8. Hans Blumenberg, "Geld oder Leben. Eine metaphorologische Studie zur Konsistenz der Philosophie Georg Simmels," *Ästhetik und Soziologie um die Jahrhundertwende: Georg Simmel* (Frankfurt: Klostermann, 1976), 127.
9. Simmel, "Eros Platonic and Modern," in Donald N. Levine, *On Individuality and Social Forms* (Chicago: University of Chicago, 1971), 243.
10. Michael Landmann, *Georg Simmel. Das individuelle Gesetz. Philosophische Exkurse* (Frankfurt: Suhrkamp, 1968), XIV.
11. "Wie überhaupt die Frau und der Eros in allen Beziehungen und Formen immer wieder sein Denken beschäftigt haben" (283) in Susman, *Erinnerungen an Georg Simmel*.
12. Theodor Litt, *Ethik der Neuzeit* (Darmstadt: Wissenschaftliche Buchgesellschaft, 1976), 175ff.

Chapter 7
Human Nature

7.1 Simmel Between Schopenhauer and Nietzsche

In his final work, *The View of Life* (1918), Simmel reflects on the place of humans in the world of life. The first essay is titled "Life as Transcendence." What Simmel means by transcendence is life's "capacity to go out beyond itself, to set its limits by reaching out beyond them; that is, beyond itself" [1]. The tension of limits introduces Simmel's idea of form: "Form means limits, contrast what is neighboring, cohesion of a periphery by means of a real or an ideal center to which, as it were, the ever on-flowing sequences of contents or processes are bent back" [2]. This language of limit and flow has obvious affinity to the writings of Simmel's contemporary philosophers of consciousness, such as Edmund Husserl, Henri Bergson, and William James. Yet Simmel's profound sociological insight is that life becomes social as it is organized first into forms, and later by these forms.

Simmel argues that human existence is continuously moving between two opposite limits. The opposition is found in all areas of human behavior, feeling, and thinking. This doctrine of opposition has greatly influenced the German catholic theologist Romano Guardini, who tried to replace the dialectic of Hegel with more communicative and dialogical dialectics. In his book *Der Gegensatz,* first published in 1925, he mentions Simmel's *The View of Life* in a brief note, but it is obvious that the whole structure of his book is an adaption of Simmel's list of oppositions imprinting human existence [3].

The idea of human nature at the turn of the century in philosophy usually referenced Hegel. In his widely received work *The Phenomenology of Spirit*, Hegel develops the idea of dialectics. Hegel was not present in Simmel's thought, maybe because he found Hegel's dialectics to be too conciliatory. Simmel instead refers to Schopenhauer and Nietzsche, comparing both in several essays. In the course of his analyses Simmel develops a number of aspects which present the feeling of life as ambivalent in view of sociality. The pivot of social experience is erotic behavior in the service of individuality. To get to Simmel's view of human

© The Author(s), under exclusive licence to Springer Nature Switzerland AG 2021
F. Fellmann, *Rethinking Georg Simmel's Social Philosophy*, SpringerBriefs in
Sociology, https://doi.org/10.1007/978-3-030-57351-5_7

nature it is appropriate to consider how Schopenhauer and Nietzsche deal with the impact of sex on human life.

We will begin with Schopenhauer, the underestimated father of modern philosophy of life. In *The World as Will and Representation*, Schopenhauer considers individuality to be a false representation of what it really is: the germline to the preservation of the species. The experience of the sexual drive gives humans a false hope of happiness. Happiness can never be attained because the fulfilment of the drive is bound to disappointment. Since life never keeps its promise of happiness to humans, it is experienced as suffering; the world "loans out" something hell-like to humans while they are on earth [4].

Humans are in the position to obtain objective knowledge through their sensations and understanding; however, the perceived world is not in agreement with their feelings. This conflicting experience pushes philosophical reflection to inquire into the reason of existence, which coincides with the inquiry into human essence. That this question, asked long before nineteenth century philosophy, has remained unanswered leads Schopenhauer to the view that human existence is absolutely contingent. Humans experience themselves as being "thrown" into the world because they experience, unlike animals living entirely in the present moment, a gap between past and present. Every question that metaphysics purportedly offers answers to (Why?, How?, and What for?) is viewed by Schopenhauer as "absolutely unfathomable" [5]. Human intelligence comes up against insoluble questions everywhere, as against the walls of Plato's cave. In this aporetic situation, philosophy is forced to reduce its exaggerated metaphysical demands for an ultimate explanation: "Philosophy can never do more than to interpret and explain what is present, to bring the essence of the world—that essence which speaks intelligibly to everyone in a concrete fashion, which is to say as a feeling—to the clear and abstract cognition of reason, and to do so in every possible respect and from every point of view" [6]. This is exactly the view of Simmel, who finds that the task of the philosophy of life is not to establish absolute certainty but to clarify immediate experiences. This analogical reasoning is not in need of further explanation. This position is regarded by some modern sociologists as a methodological weakness, but they overlook the enlightening force of intuition, which has nothing to do with speculation. For Simmel, intuition is what the American anthropologist has called "thick description" and needs no argument.

Schopenhauer called his philosophy immanent. Only interpretation and clarification of what is immediately given deliver reliable results; however, there is no "pure reason" in what is immediately given. For Schopenhauer, individuality is dominated by a will with a strong need, which can ultimately never be satisfied. The "primacy of the will in self-consciousness" brings an end to every attempt to justify epistemically the fabric of the social world. Schopenhauer refuted Leibniz's optimistic theodicy angrily as an unethical way of thinking and termed the world "the worst possible," as its existence depends entirely upon cosmic chance. The "Logodicy" (i.e., the justification of reason given to humans by God) was countered by Schopenhauer with agnosticism.

Schopenhauer holds spatio-temporal individuation to be an illusion. Personal identity does not result from the logical I as the highest point of knowledge but from the elementary striving for self-preservation penetrating every aspect of life. The prototype of self-preservation is, according to Schopenhauer, not hunger but love in its animalistic form of sexuality. To make sexuality human, Schopenhauer propagated the "negation of the will to live" that leads to Nirvana, the Buddhist experience of Nothingness. Schopenhauer, curiously, says little about Nothing (*Nichts*), but describes the world in the state of affirmation of the will. The groundlessness and constant view of the abyss lead to an unforeseen intensification of the feeling of life. This is the paradox in Schopenhauer's philosophy that makes him the first representative of modernity: the real dialectic of negation and affirmation of the will to live cannot be resolved by reason.

This concept of the will has nothing to do with freedom but represents a purely biological and psychological drive that spans all creatures. Because humans are driven by a will that is "blind," they feel themselves as one with all other human creatures. If one sets aside metaphysical speculations, the significant insight remains that the anonymous will to live is the source of personal identity: "At bottom it is the will that is spoken of whenever 'I' appears in a judgment. Thus, it is the true and final point of unity of consciousness, and the bond of all its functions and acts; it does not itself, however, belong to the intellect, but is only its root, source, and controller" [7]. For Schopenhauer, the will to live "is something that is taken for granted: it is a prius of the intellect itself. We ourselves are the will to live, and therefore we must live, well or ill." The will to live can never be broken, but it can be made clear by the unhindered appearance of the will. This results in pure, or as it is termed, "intuitive knowledge," which no longer works in the service of the will. The will is able to recognize itself in intuitive knowledge.

This astounding turn of thinking can be considered the philosophical basis of Simmel's theory of individuality. Although the human experiences him or herself as an identical subject, identity points to a deeper layer of life connecting all creatures. Identity that is fueled by the intense feeling of living comes from body image as the maximum of personal reality. This idea is reinforced by sexuality. Because sexual desire is concentrated on intercourse with a partner, the principle of individuation becomes the principle of reciprocity. The presence of the other is not expressed in rational knowledge but in the pain and joy the lovers experience together. Schopenhauer thus opens the way for the emergence of individuality from erotic love—a way that connects Schopenhauer with Simmel, who establishes relational sociology on intimate relations.

Before turning to Simmel's conclusion, it is helpful to consider his view of Nietzsche's philosophy. Nietzsche's influence made the place of humans more unpleasant: on the one hand, there was the loneliness of the isolated individual, and on the other, the insatiable desire for erotic communication. Nietzsche heightened the tension into a liberating madness. He fooled himself into believing there was a community of love that he never reached, neither as a thinker nor as a man. His radicalization of anthropology changed the "will to live" into the "will to power"—of course not yet understood as political power. The power that Nietzsche dreamed of is the power of fantasy, from which he derived an "aesthetic justification of the world" in the *Birth of Tragedy*:

> For the more I become aware of those all-powerful natural artistic impulses and the fervent yearning for illusion contained in them, the desire to be redeemed through appearances, the more I feel myself pushed to the metaphysical assumption that the true being and the primordial oneness, ever-suffering and entirely contradictory, constantly uses the delightful vision, the joyful illusion, to redeem itself; we are compelled to experience this illusion, totally caught up in it and constituted by it, as the truly non-existent, that is, as a continuous development in time, space, and causality, in other words, as empirical reality [8].

Who does Nietzsche want to justify by means of the beautiful appearance? Not the unknowable God of Christianity whom he declared as dead; rather, the beautiful appearance was to justify the Greek Olympians, who were very similar to humans. Opposed to reason, the creative productivity of the artist, who shapes his or her own world, brings about an agreement between the gods and humans, leading Nietzsche to write: "The same impulse which summons art into life as the seductive replenishment for further living and the completion of existence also gave rise to the Olympian world, in which the Hellenic 'Will' held before itself a transfiguring mirror. In this way, the gods justify the lives of men, because they themselves live it—that is the only satisfactory theodicy!" [9]. By situating the Olympians on the same level as artists, Nietzsche transforms negative anthropology into aesthetic anthropology. Both humans and gods work toward overcoming contingency by means of the pleasurable appearance of art.

But the following question still remains: Is the pleasurable appearance enough to provide justification for humans in view of the self-provoked horrors existing in the world? When crimes increase in monstrosity to the point of threatening the existence of humanity itself, aesthetic justification is pushed to its absolute limit. Justification thus becomes merely compensatory. This may have been felt by those thinkers who asked the more than rhetorical question: Is it even possible to still write a poem after Auschwitz? To answer questions such as this one, one needs an authority that transcends aesthetic belief and opens up a dimension of reflection that goes forth from out of the abysses and contradictions of human reality itself. The search for this authority, which Nietzsche experienced toward the end of the nineteenth century as the tragedy of the aristocratic spirit, has produced a difficult task for twentieth century social philosophy. How can the will to power bring the self-destructive modern times to reason and justify individuals despite their exaggerated will to self-preservation?

Simmel seems to have wondered about this question as well. His position between Schopenhauer and Nietzsche is concluding in the following passage:

> The conviction of the worthlessness of life and the conviction of the worthiness of life … these convictions are not theoretical knowledge but the expression of the fundamental qualities of souls, and they cannot be reconciled in a higher unity, just as no Being is identical with another. Because the value of what may be called their synthesis consists in precisely this: that mankind experiences a tension of life-feelings. Therefore, the unity of these convictions can be attained in another dimension than in their objective content: in the subject, who sees both. When we feel the vibration of spiritual Dasein in these oppositions,

the soul extends itself . . . until life's desperation and rejoicing as the poles of the soul's own breadth, own strength, and its own fullness can be gathered and enjoyed [10].

In other words, human experience is inexorably conflictual but on a higher level most meaningful when in the service of humanity.

Concerning the principle of individuality, we have seen that Simmel moves between the pessimistic worldview of Arthur Schopenhauer and the optimistic will to power of Friedrich Nietzsche. The starting point for both is the yearning for an absolute goal that is unattainable. Whereas for Schopenhauer individual life entails suffering and the salvation from suffering is the denial of the will to live, Nietzsche views life as the progress of cultural evolution. Simmel takes something from both thinkers; he points out the ambivalence of modernity: humans have become alienated from the primordial state of life, which is evident in the disclosure of intimacy. His cultural sociology explains the advancement of human nature using a circular process of real and ideal exchange and hence avoids the clash of culture that has since become an urgent problem. Simmel's view of the process of individuation provides useful suggestions for how to preserve the one world that we now live in despite the plurality of cultural traditions.

7.2 Philosophical Anthropology

The emergence of philosophical anthropology in the twentieth century does not explicitly refer to Simmel. Nevertheless, Simmel's image of man can be seen as a subliminal source of modern anthropology. This becomes clear if one looks at the main representant of anthropological philosophy in Germany, Max Scheler, who was Simmel's student for two terms at Humboldt University in Berlin. Scheler also frequented Simmel's private lectures at his cultural salon. Nietzsche's attack on humanism was highly *en vogue*. Simmel and Scheler both tried to create a philosophy of life to correct the rationalistic trends of objective culture in Western civilization.

Scheler's work *The Human Place in the Cosmos* (1927) can be called the founding document of modern philosophical anthropology. Scheler's method was semi-empirical. He used the results of biological and behavioral research yet was not content with a description of humans that was merely an enumeration of characteristics. Rather, he interpreted human characteristics in the light of the late idealistic *Weltanschauung*. As a result of the reduction of instincts, humans are subjected to their moods in an uncontrollable fashion, contrary to the rigid animal behavior pattern. This is particularly manifested in the case of sexual life.

Human dignity is obviously grounded in the ability to control drives. Scheler ascribes this ability to "spirit," a principle contradictory to mere life. He derives the "exceptional position" of humans from this: they have a "world-open" (*weltoffen*) nature that nears the divine. In Scheler's emphatic language:

The human being is a creature that, by virtue of its spirit, can take an ascetic attitude toward its fervent and vibrating life—the human being can suppress and repress its own drive impulses, and it can refuse to give them their sustenance in the form of perceivable images and representations. By comparison to animals, who always say 'Yes' to reality—even when they fear and flee—the human being is the 'Nay-sayer,' he is an ascetic of life; he is an eternal protester against all mere reality [11].

Scheler's negativism is quite unique. He interprets saying "no" to natural drives as the liberation of the human to spirit (*Geist*). It is not surprising, then, that Scheler actually turns against the "negative theory of humans" in Schopenhauer and in Freud's later works. But this is obviously a misunderstanding of his own position. The negation of an urge, which itself is an expression of lack, does not actually eliminate the urge, but strengthens it and raises it to the level of consciousness. Thus the "problem of human nature"—which Scheler classifies as the tension-filled relation between being determined by drives and ideal values—remains unsolved. Scheler's anthropology is a heroic yet ultimately failed attempt to balance conflicting powers. Here, Scheler is lacking Simmel's lifeline of social philosophy.

Philosophical anthropology was most at odds with Simmel's concept of culture in Arnold Gehlen's classic entitled *Man: His Nature and Place In the World* (1940). Gehlen considers humans to be biologically "deficient beings" who possess, in contrast to animals, only weak instincts and no highly specialized organs. This exceptional position is the precondition of cultural activity. Humans compensate for their lack through rules of behavior and institutions. But institutional relief happens, so to say, behind the backs of the individuals who are dependent on their changing feelings and moods. According to Gehlen, humans are not only biologically deficient, but also mentally deficient creatures. Far from contributing to the stabilization of social institutions, subjectivity works silently toward its own destruction.

For Gehlen, particularly, exaggerated self-reflection represents a danger for modern individual life. Although he stresses the human need for self-confidence, he does not believe that it is obtained through intersubjectivity; rather, it can be acquired through social institutions, because only institutions can provide external stabilization and protect society from the destructive tendencies of subjectivism. Gehlen's anti-subjectivism nearly eliminates subjective experience, making personality a mere function of the institution. Gehlen's philosophy of institutions points to hierarchical structures in its social and political consequences and is incompatible with Simmel's principle of intersubjectivity as the basis of social organizations.

Theodor Adorno followed Gehlen in rejecting relativism, but his thinking was more dialectical. He published *Negative Dialectics* in 1966. "Negative Dialectics" means the destruction of the tightly held principle of the unity of consciousness from the classical philosophy of transcendental idealism. Adorno's model of the human mind does away with every sort of determinism, in any case the determinism of marginality and nonconformity of "antiheroes." Adorno also held the question of the meaning of life to be outdated: "When a desperate man who wants to kill himself asks one who tries to talk him out of it about the point of living, the helpless helper will be at a loss to name one" [12]. If one takes the "antinomic" structure of reason uncovered by Kant seriously, then it becomes apparent that Adorno's discussion of Simmel's concept of conflict destroys Simmel's hope for reconciliation. Society and individuality both become, in their reciprocity, false and even violent. Adorno's attitude toward Simmel was ambivalent. While he adopted Simmel's forms of sociation, he also criticized sharply Simmel's intuitive view of everyday phenomena. This ambivalence seems to be due to the fact that Adorno like Simmel is still rooted in the *Lebensanschauung* of the late nineteenth century wavering between realism and idealism.

German philosophical anthropology is in agreement with several important aspects of Simmel's phenomenology of social life. Simmel's concern was not how social institutions function but how individuals create the very forms of sociality in interaction between two limits, which separate humans from both animal life and divine life. Consequently, Simmel's image of man shows several layers of personality. This model is in modern secular societies timelier than ever before. In addition, a new threat has been added to societal problems: the use of genetic technology to manipulate the biological constitution of humans. The more humans are able to reconstruct their biological constitution, and the more the act of reproduction becomes a technical act in the laboratory, the more difficult it becomes to understand what it really means to be a human. In Goethe's *Faust* the creation of "homunculus" evokes the complicity of the devil, a topic Simmel dealt with in his *Goethe* monograph. Today, the anthropological question increasingly becomes a question of justification, and philosophical anthropology has to take into account synthetic biology.

7.3 Existential Justification

"Every being intellectually inferior to man (*untergeistiges Wesen*) is beyond the question of value and right, it is quite simply. The human's elevated position and distress can be summed up in the formula that he must justify his own being" [13]. This statement by Simmel leaves one with much to consider. If humans, in contrast to animals, must justify their own being, then justification cannot simply be what we normally think of as "justification." Normally, to justify oneself means to offer explanatory or apologetic reasons for individual acts that are thought to be incomprehensible or unacceptable. This understanding of justification makes no sense in reference to human beings, because no one needs to apologize for his or her own existence or inborn character. The necessity of justification suggests another meaning that has been lost in the current discourse—a meaning that can only be reclaimed by reflecting on the history of ideas.

"Justification" is currently used in analytic philosophy as a rationale. "Epistemic justification" refers to argumentation that should lead to "true knowledge." Whereas most analytic philosophers employ a correspondence conception of truth and consider justification as a means to get to truth, Simmel, who was not a trained logician, confounds epistemic and semantic questions. Truth thus loses its absoluteness and is reduced to "justified belief" within a system of mutually supportive statements. Since the connections within the argumentation as a whole remain unfounded, processes of justification are forced to refer to normative assumptions. Without such assumptions, the alleged relation between justification and truth would be inexplicable. According to Simmel, justification ultimately always leads to the question: What should we believe? The answer can only be given by an "ethics of belief" pointing to the oftentimes unconscious presupposition that a theological meaning lies behind the purely cognitive conception of justification.

It was William James who combined the theological and the epistemological meaning of justification. In his book *The Will to Believe* James attempts to defend the rationality of religious faith, even though he is lacking sufficient evidence of the existence of a personal God. James states in the introduction: "I have brought with me tonight something like a sermon on justification by faith to read to you,—I mean an essay in justification of faith, a defense of our right to adopt a believing attitude in religious matters, in spite of the fact that our merely logical intellect may not have been coerced. 'The Will to Believe,' accordingly, is the title of my paper" [14].

With his announcement of a "sermon on justification by faith," James is referring to the Paulinian *justificatio sola fide* but then inconspicuously shifts from the pastoral discourse to philosophical argumentation and speaks about the "justification of faith." In this way the theological meaning of justification shifted to theoretical argumentation, which, then, could no longer be described using the word "faith." Faith is transformed into a believing attitude and James thus arrives at belief as the guiding idea of pragmatism.

James' central argument in *The Will to Believe* is that the evidence for whether or not certain beliefs are true depends upon first adopting those beliefs. As an example, James argues that it can be rational to have faith in one's own ability to accomplish tasks that require confidence. Importantly, James points out that this is the case even for scientific inquiry. He then argues that, like belief in one's own ability to accomplish a difficult task, religious faith can also be rational even if one lacks evidence for the truth of divine revelation at the time. "Justification through belief" is based on justification by practical works, which James extended to mental works such as scientific research. But his use of Paulinist expressions cannot hide the fact that he is dealing with a secularization of theological ways of thinking. Justification thus stands for the worldly form of salvation of humans by humans: salvation obviously not only in the sense of forgiveness but in the sense of reconciling desire's dissonance with shared pleasures. Like cultural Protestantism, James represents pragmatism as a quasi-religious way of salvation brought about by social interaction as described in Simmel's relational sociology.

In contrast to James' pragmatism, the German protestant theologian Karl Barth was in search of a new absolute. In his famous commentary on Paul, *The Epistle to the Romans*, Barth severs the certainty of belief from the world of cultural life and attributes the religious impact to God as "entirely Other" [15]. If a reconciliation and salvation for humans really does exist, then it can only be through God's mercy, which allows no comparison with worldly justice. For believers who rely entirely on the mercy of God, reason appears to be worthless—even unreasonable. In the "paradox of belief" the unknown God reveals himself to humans as fundamentally different from the "shape of the world"—both physical and mental shapes.

The self-named "dialectical" theology presented a strong challenge to social philosophy. For philosophy the unsurpassable boundaries in its efforts to reconcile the individual with society became evident. It was clear that the absolute justification of human existence from logical reasons is just as impossible as the ultimate justification of knowledge. Considering the hopeless state of the world, the only thing remaining for humans, in the view of dialectical theology, is the radical negation of all temporal experience, as well as the negation of the claims of validity of time-transcending truths of reason. Both forms of appearances of God, as court and mercy, go beyond the horizon of human reason and point to the unfathomable depths of a divinity that is a paradox in and of itself. Thus, a theological concept of justification was established, which fundamentally did away with every positive representation. This naturally does not mean that the demand for rationality and autonomy will be abandoned. What was required is rather an expansion of Logos, which circles within itself. Sought after was an open form of rationality that considers the subjective alongside the objective side of life.

When Barth speaks of Eros, which he does at length in *The Epistle to the Romans*, he was obviously not only thinking of Plato, but also of the libido according to Freud's controversial doctrine of sexuality. Barth appears to know instinctually that more was behind Eros than his invectives against Eros admit to. He himself warns of an underestimation of the power of Eros [16]. Should Eros really not show a way to redemption? Perhaps Eros is not so different from religious faith, which had its beginning in the fear of God and ended with his love.

In the light of dialectical theology all attempts by modern theories of mind to provide personal identity and self-certainty prove to be insufficient. Justification is, in opposition to rational argumentation, an idea that points to the multi-dimensionality of human subjective experience and emotional intelligence. In the words of Ludwig Wittgenstein, "What people accept as a justification—is shown by how they think and live" [17]. If justification by Logos is no longer available, only Eros can take up God's position. In erotic love, man and woman both become conscious of who they are and what they actually expect from life. This knowledge is granted through the recognition by the loved partner. With regard to recognition, we cannot deny another the recognition of his achievements, even if we do not like him as a person. Love, in contrast, is the acceptance of the other regardless of his achievements. Unlike recognition, love is and remains an occurrence, and the lovers will never know the reason for it. Love can only be explained, if at all, through love, which is why lovers ask "Do you love me or not?" and never "Why do you love me?". In this way intimate relations is the only form of justification that is made up entirely of reciprocity. In sexual unification, each partner is both subject and object, at least according to the concept of erotic justification.

Looking back to Simmel's concept of existential justification, it becomes clear that his philosophy of religion is near to cultural Protestantism and that the impact of Eros in social life is the core meaning of Simmel's principle of reciprocity. For Simmel—whose methodology is in accordance with William James' Radical

Empiricism (James and Simmel both show similarities to Bergson's concept of life)—personal identity is always a relation from individual to individual. Without this relation personal identity would lose its stability. Intimate relations cannot develop in pure action schemes because love represents—as the erotic in general—the intersubjective creation of meaning. This is why it follows an emotional schema in which the parameters must be continually adjusted in every concrete relationship. The schema of Eros forms the basis of all representations and articulations in erotic love. Eros mediates between the lovers' expectations uniquely: it differs from mere functional relationships because it is unconditional. Even in modern integral relationships where each partner is equal, love still cannot be rationally planned.

Simmel's principle of individuality, which includes all dimensions of intersubjectivity, confirms the justificatory function of Eros. As Simmel puts it, "Genuine erotic life in fact flows naturally in individual channels." Other than the action schema, which calls for an abstract and genderless subject, the schema of Eros turns the lovers into whole persons who cannot be divided into a chain of single actions. Of course, actions also belong to loving. But actions performed "out of love" transcend behavior patterns. They develop confidence, which arises out of intimacy: persons rely on others, on themselves, and on the whole world. This confidence delivers "ontological security" (Anthony Giddens) that cannot be reached through self-determination alone. The belief in love functions as a sentiment binding men and women together. This is the elementary root of community that human freedom can always return to, because in Eros, despite all fixation on the momentary maximizing of pleasure, there is a belief in the common future which is in no way inferior to the formal structure of faith in God.

As long as Eros and Logos remain connected to each other in love, the individual is despite all weaknesses and contradictions justified by a fundamental confidence in the partner, which is constitutive for the principle of reciprocity. The alleged incompatibility of men and women is a result of the separation of Logos from Eros, or of reason from life; and all forms of alienation are a result of the smashing of erotic love into fragments of sexuality. This applies to traditional forms of arranged marriages and modern forms of "partner-swapping" alike. Of course, modern humans cannot manage without the division of labor; but the objective separation of areas is only bearable if the whole is maintained in a common scheme of presentation, which individuals need if they are to freely exist in society. If the alienation of modern life can be overcome, then this is really only through the scheme of Eros, which allows access to the deeper layers of personality. Here, Simmel's view of the vital character of erotic life as a continuous flux of reciprocal interaction—like a swift-flowing river, never stopping—was trendsetting. In Simmel's view, personality is molded by the interaction between the outer formal pattern of behavior and the inner subjective state of mind—two sides of life that are often conflictual. This ambivalent image of humans as wanderers between two frontiers has made Simmel a founder of relational sociology in a phenomenological key and at the same time an outstanding cultural philosopher of the modern ages.

References

1. Simmel, *The View of Life: Four Metaphysical Essays with Journal Aphorisms* (Chicago: University of Chicago Press), 10.
2. Simmel, *The View of Life,* 11.
3. Romano Guardini, *Der Gegensatz* (Wiesbaden: Rauch, 1925). See page 39 for the brief note.
4. Arthur Schopenhauer, The World as Will and Representation, Vol. 2, trans. E.F.J. Payne (New York: Dover Publications, 1966), 747.
5. Schopenhauer, *The World as Will and Representation*, Vol. 2, 823.
6. Arthur Schopenhauer, *The World as Will and Representation*, Vol. 1, trans. E.F.J. Payne (New York: Dover Publications, 1966), 376.
7. Schopenhauer, *The World as Will and Representation*, Vol. 2, 334.
8. Friedrich Nietzsche, *The Birth of Tragedy* (London: Penguin Books, 2003).
9. Nietzsche, *The Birth of Tragedy*, 36.
10. Simmel, *Schopenhauer und Nietzsche* (Hamburg: Tredition Classics, 2012). Translation by Ferdinand Fellmann.
11. Max Scheler, *The Human Place in the Cosmos*, trans. Manfred S. Frings (Evanston, IL: Northwestern University Press, 2009), 39.
12. Theodor Adorno, *Negative Dialectics* (New York: Continuum, 1966), 376.
13. Simmel, *Goethe* (Leipzig: Klinkhardt and Biermann, 1913), 264.
14. William James, *The Will to Believe and Other Essays in Popular Philosophy, and Human Immortality* (New York: Dover Publications, 1956), 1.
15. *The Epistle to the Romans* (London: Oxford University Press), 134.
16. Ibid., 434.
17. *Philosophical Investigations*, transl. Anscombe, 1953, §325.

Epilogue

Now, at the end of this book, I would like to present myself to the reader. I am an emeritus professor of philosophy who taught at several European universities. I remained devoted to the continental philosophical tradition despite the predominance of analytic philosophy that was at that time in Germany rather dogmatic but has since become softer in the form of philosophy of mind. I was introduced to the work of Simmel by a professor, the renowned German Philosopher Hans Blumenberg. His thought was deeply influenced by Simmel and Husserl [1]. My book has a clear German imprint, which might make it uninteresting for American readers at first sight. I, to the contrary, consider my perspective an exceptional way of seeing that can arouse explorative curiosity in open-minded social researchers.

The impact of Simmel's ideas on my own thought is noticeable in my philosophy of history, and later on in my philosophy of life. My work covers a wide spectrum of cultural anthropology and focuses especially on erotic love and male-female polarity. Following modern psychoanalysis, I emphasize the role of eroticism in the making of the human mind. Since 2000, my thinking has been influenced by the evolutionary side of human life. To the question of evolutionary biology, "How have we become humans?", I have given an unconventional answer: More than patterns of behavior, the subjective experience of erotic relations has formed human personality. Eroticism as an essential precondition for human evolution is explained in my book *The Couple. Intimate Relations in a New key* (2016) and in several articles in scientific journals [2].

This point of view directed my attention to the erotic undercurrent of Simmel's cultural philosophy and his life/form dualism. I have exposed this current in diverse entries of the German *Simmel Handbuch* (2018). In Germany, I am generally considered a philosopher of Eros in affinity with Simmel. To clarify the shift of philosophy from logical thinking to bodily wisdom, I coined the new term "*Erosoph*", English: "Erosopher" in place of "Philosopher". In the new term, Eros figures as subject and object, i.e., Eros loves wisdom and is the epitome of wisdom [3]. This does not mean that I support "pansexualism" (the critical response to Freud's psychoanalysis); rather, I think that erotic and aesthetic experience are

F. Fellmann, *Rethinking Georg Simmel's Social Philosophy*, SpringerBriefs in Sociology, https://doi.org/10.1007/978-3-030-57351-5

always at work in human culture. Consequently, I am convinced that even if postmodern individualism were to break down all social structures, intimate relations would remain the ultimate means of social cohesion.

In view of this background one may ask what will become of sociology in the future. In my opinion, the borders between sociology, psychology, ethnology, etc., are disappearing. Is this the end of sociology? Yes, in its traditional form as an independent discipline dealing exclusively with the so-called "social facts". No, in the way Simmel dealt with phenomena of social life, focusing specifically on the method of genetic phenomenology. The genetic method enables one to lay open the deeper layers of human existence that are pre-reflective, passive, and anonymous, though nonetheless active as in sexual life. Interest in the ongoing process of social change, which is nowadays going faster and faster, and attention to new matters of social research create a new style of presentation particular to each. This new style is fragmentary, personal, and uses everyday language, as is common in feuilletons and magazines. Simmel also published many of his subtle observations in Berlin newspapers. Though Simmel was reproached during his time by scholars for lacking systematic generalization, this now turns out to be the strength of his intuitive reasoning and writings about the world of social life.

References

1. See Blumenberg, "Geld oder Leben" and *Phänomenologische Schriften: 1981–1988* (Frankfurt: Suhrkamp, 2018).
2. See Ferdinand Fellmann and Rebecca Walsh, "From Sexuality to Eroticism" and Fellmann, "Eroticism: Why it Still Matters," *Psychology* 07: 976–983 (2016).
3. Ferdinand Fellmann, *Erosoph. Eine philosophische Autobiographie* (Würzburg: Königshausen and Neumann, 2019).